MIRACLES DO HAPPEN

Fela and Felix Rosenbloom were both born in Poland in the early 1920s. They grew up in the same street in Lodz and became sweethearts, before their lives were devastated by the Holocaust. After the war, they reunited, married, and moved to Paris, France. They migrated to Australia with their son Henry in 1952, and settled in Melbourne, where their second son, John, was born. Felix died in 1995.

MIRACLES DO HAPPEN

Fela and Felix Rosenbloom

SCRIBE
Melbourne • London

Scribe Publications.
18–20 Edward St, Brunswick, Victoria 3056, Australia
2 John St, Clerkenwell, London, WC1N 2ES, United Kingdom

First published by the authors 1994
First published by Scribe in this edition 2017

Copyright © Fela and Felix Rosenbloom 2017

All rights reserved. Without limiting the rights under copyright reserved above, no part of this publication may be reproduced, stored in or introduced into a retrieval system, or transmitted, in any form or by any means (electronic, mechanical, photocopying, recording or otherwise) without the prior written permission of the publishers of this book.

The moral rights of the authors have been asserted.

Printed and bound in Australia by Griffin Press

The paper this book is printed on is certified against the Forest Stewardship Council® Standards. Griffin Press holds FSC chain of custody certification SGS-COC-005088. FSC promotes environmentally responsible, socially beneficial and economically viable management of the world's forests.

Scribe Publications is committed to the sustainable use of natural resources and the use of paper products made responsibly from those resources.

9781925322309 (Australian edition)
9781925548525 (e-book)

A CiP entry for this title is available from the National Library of Australia.

scribepublications.com.au
scribepublications.co.uk

*To our children, Henry and John, their spouses,
Margot and Kathy, and our grandchildren,
Miriam, Max, David, and Noah*

Contents

Publisher's note   ix

Part One

Fela   1

Part Two

Felix   43

Publisher's note

My father originally prepared this book for his close family and friends. He was working on it when he was suddenly diagnosed with cancer, and amid the shock of dealing with this I helped him finalise the text before he printed a small quantity in 1994.

Dad died not long after, in May 1995, and this small book became a poignant and treasured piece of personal testimony by him and my mother.

Inevitably, as the book was passed around, more people got to hear of it and asked if it was possible to receive a copy. I arranged for a couple of small reprints over the years, but secretly yearned to publish it professionally. My mother, who is now in her nineties and is an intensely private person, has always been traumatised by her experience of the Holocaust, so it never seemed possible to bring it to the public. However, a year or so ago, I happened to be reminiscing about the book with her, and I was very surprised when she urged me to publish it.

When my brother, John, heard of this, he also gave his consent, and later helped me a great deal by checking the dates and details of a vast number of historical facts and events, and by suggesting corrections to the spelling of placenames and personal names. I should explain here that our family's surname, originally spelled 'Rozenblum', was changed by deed poll at my request several years after we arrived in Australia to 'Rosenbloom'.

So here it is, more than twenty years after it was first released. I have copy-edited it lightly, and inserted a few footnotes where that seemed relevant. It is a remarkable joint memoir, which speaks for itself.

Henry Rosenbloom

PART ONE

Fela

Preface

I SURVIVED World War II by a sheer miracle. When peace came at last, I still lived in constant fear. Time and time again, I asked myself: *Is it true that I am alive? Am I the same person?* After a long inner turmoil, I came to the conclusion that I had lost my previous self in the gas ovens of Auschwitz, and that a second life was given to me only to prolong my sufferings — I had to come to terms with my new self. However, the nightmare of Auschwitz never left me and became a part of me.

In 1974, I was asked to contribute the story of my war experiences to a *Yizkor Buch* (commemorative book) called *Jewish Lodz*. My story, together with a photograph of a group of women, camp inmates, appeared on page 143.

Then, in 1987, I was approached by a journalist from *The Age* newspaper, Anna Murdoch, who had been working on a large article about Holocaust survivors in Melbourne. She asked me if I would agree to be interviewed by her. I consented, and we had two long sessions together.

As I told my story to Anna, I relived the horrors of Auschwitz. I felt as if my veins were bursting and the bleeding could not be stopped. Anna was deeply moved by my story, but I had many sleepless nights before and after the interviews. An edited version of the interviews appeared in the 'Saturday Extra' section of *The Age* of 22 August 1987, in an article titled 'Survivors of the Holocaust'.

When my husband and sons insisted that I write my memoirs, I felt that so many books had been written about the Holocaust that I had nothing new to add. However, being the sole survivor of my whole family, I owe it to the memory of my father, mother, brothers, and sister, who perished along with six million Jews, to tell my story.

Chapter One

MY FATHER, Chil Chaim Perelman, was born in 1888 in the small village of Bieliny in south-central Poland, about twenty kilometres east of the regional centre, Kielce, where his parents had an orchard. He once told us children that the orchard was so big that he could gallop on a horse around the fruit trees. I remember him as a handsome man with brown eyes, curly brown hair, a nice short nose, and a lovely, pink complexion. He always had a beard, and wore a cap and a dark Orthodox outfit.

When father married my mother, he was eighteen years old. He had no profession at the time. To earn a living, he started a cartage business. He bought carts and horses, and employed two people, distributing all sorts of goods from factories to warehouses and to large hardware and china shops. Some of the shops belonged to our relatives. Father was a very trusted person, and was given the keys to all the shops he serviced. He was a very good provider for his family until he had a stroke of bad luck. One after another, his horses died of food poisoning and, as a consequence, his business collapsed. That happened in 1928–1929.* Times were very tough then, and he struggled to make a living. He used to get up in the early hours of the morning and travel to nearby country farms to buy dairy products, which he sold on to shopkeepers.

My mother, Chaja Ruchla, was born in 1885 in the village of Nowa Słupia, eleven kilometres east of Bieliny. Her maiden name was Cukier, and her father was the local cantor. My mother must have been pretty as a girl. She had beautiful green eyes and dark hair, turning grey, always covered by a wig, as was the custom of Orthodox married women. My girlfriends used to remark that my mother's face and expressive, longish nose were like those of an aristocrat. As long as I could remember, mother's face had deep lines — which used to amaze me, because father, by contrast, had an exceptionally fresh complexion. At the same time, there was something majestic about her appearance; one could not help respecting her.

Mother once showed me her wedding dress, which she kept in a drawer all those years. It was a black, beautiful lace dress. I was astonished by how very slim my mother must have been as a bride. She told me that her future mother-in-law was afraid that, being so very slim, my mother would not be able to bear children. Even after giving birth to nine children, she stayed slim and tall. Her wrinkled, sad face gave the impression of a person in sorrow. This was most certainly

---

* There is a ghetto record showing that Fela's parents moved into their flat in Młynarska St in Lodz in May 1918. This could well be around the time they moved from Bieliny to Lodz.

due to the fact that she had lost five children, all of them born before me.

I can vaguely remember the death of an older brother. But it was the death of my sister Blime (Bluma), when I was six years old, that left a lasting impression on me. Blime was a very pretty young lady who wore pigtails, and she was liked by everyone. She died in hospital at the age of sixteen, due to complications after the removal of her appendix. At the time of her death, Blime was engaged and soon to be married.

The people next door took care of me and my two brothers while my parents made arrangements for the burial of Blime. For days, there was an atmosphere of great distress, not only in our flat, but throughout the whole apartment block. All the neighbours were close to us and shared our misfortune. Now, being a mother myself, I can understand how my mother felt, losing one child after another.

Not long after Blime's death, mother gave birth to a baby girl. I can still recall the midwife who entered our apartment, the first cry of the newborn baby, and someone shouting *Mazel tov* to my father, waiting outside. In accordance with Jewish Orthodox tradition, father only then entered the room. The baby girl was named Bayle (Bella). She was the ninth and the last child of my parents.

I loved my little sister very much, but I do not remember much about her childhood. I must have been too busy at school. As I grew older, I wanted Bayle to have things that I did not have as a child. As soon as I began to earn money, I bought some pink woollen material and gave it to a dressmaker, Mr Fuks, who made up a beautiful dress for my sister. Mrs Fuks also had a daughter of Bayle's age, and the two girls were playmates. I wanted Bayle to get a higher education. I planned to work hard and pay for it.

When the war broke out, Bayle was nine years old. I left the Lodz ghetto in April 1941, on my way to a German labour camp. Bayle was in tears, begging me to come back soon. She hoped that the war would be over in six months' time. I never saw my family again. When I left, my brother Dovid (David) was very ill, due to malnutrition. He died soon afterwards, in May 1941. Father also starved to death in the ghetto, several months later, in January 1942. In April 1942, my mother, my younger brother, Zelig, and Bayle were all deported to Chełmno, where they perished. All my life I grieve for Bayle. She was so young, so good, so innocent.

I was a very lively child, and prone to laugh on any occasion. Someone just had to hold up a finger in front of me and I would burst into laughter. I also used to have a lot of fun with my brothers and sister, especially when we made up and performed little plays together. I had a habit of singing most of the time while I was inside the house. Because I sang in Polish, a language my parents hated, they strongly disapproved of it. They were deeply religious and self-conscious Jews. They knew the history of anti-Semitic outbursts and pogroms in Poland. Their personal experiences had left them with an enduring distaste for the language of their oppressors, and they insisted on only Yiddish being spoken at home.

My parents were very strict Orthodox Jews; our home

adhered to all the religious rules. Mother, especially, was so strict that it made me very unhappy. On the Sabbath I was not allowed to do anything, and that made me at times discontented. I was different. I was in conflict with myself and did not know how things would work out. Mother behaved as though she was the wife of a rabbi. Every Friday evening all the neighbours would look through our windows to see when my mother lit the Sabbath candles. Then they would follow and light theirs. They relied on her and trusted her.

Although my parents were not very happy with my not very religious and sometimes rebellious behaviour, they loved me very much. Orthodox Jews do not show their feelings towards their children. They do not hug them or kiss them. However, I knew that they, especially mother, were very proud of me. I overheard them once saying to each other, 'Don't we have a lovely daughter?' On some occasions, when I went out with my girlfriends, mother would hide in a corner to check how I looked, and when I saw her she would just disappear.

Two incidents during my childhood left a lasting impression on my psychological development.

One day, I was at home when a stranger knocked at the door and asked about my mother. She was out, so he left a calling card and came back later. When they met, I was astonished to hear my mother addressing the man in German — which meant she assumed that he was not Jewish. Mother must have been surprised to be told in Yiddish that the man she was talking to was her brother. It turned out that they had not seen each other for twenty years. After they embraced, the details of his life emerged.

Hieronim, as he called himself, had been fairly well educated for his times. As a young man he had worked as a Hebrew teacher, but he had the good luck to make a wealthy match, which gave him the means to set up and run a chemical plant. Now, with orders coming in from Lodz, he had arrived on a business trip, and had decided to look up his sister. During all the previous years, my uncle had never written us a letter. I think that what really had kept him and my mother apart was religion. Although both of them had the same upbringing, my uncle became a non-practising Jew, while my mother remained strictly Orthodox and deeply religious.

Not long afterwards, a woman came to us asking for the cantor's daughter, meaning my mother. That was the first time, but not the last, I heard that my grandfather had been a cantor. From then on, my mother would bore me endlessly with tales of what a highly respected and famous man her father had been. 'If you knew, my child, the stock you come from, as fine as silk and satin', was a constant lament of hers. One of her favourite stories was how her father, the cantor, travelling around to different synagogues, would come down from his coach directly into a chair, so positioned that his feet would not touch the ground.

Despite my discomfort at being constantly told about mother's worthy forebears, the message sank in, and I became immensely proud of my family's supposedly high reputation.

I was determined to live up to the high expectations my mother held for me, in all my behaviour and actions. To people I came in contact with, I probably started to seem aloof — a trait of character I have never really been able to shed. By the time I was a teenager, people were accusing me of being 'different', an accusation I was to hear again in Auschwitz and even later in life. It was especially hurtful to me when my own mother began to reproach me, saying that I behaved as if I was 'the daughter of Poznański'. To the Jews of Lodz, Poznański, a Jew and owner of a huge textile factory, was thought of and envied as if he were a Rothschild.

One day in 1933, as I was standing in front of our apartment block with my childhood friend and neighbour Roysa, I noticed some new faces on the first-floor balcony across the street. Among them was a girl of our age, reading a newspaper. Those people had probably just moved in. I was happy to see a change of tenants. The previous ones had been Poles who used to show their anti-Semitism openly. My girlfriend and I decided to get acquainted with the girl on the balcony.

From the moment I entered their apartment, I felt at home and welcomed by the Rozenblum family. However, my girlfriend Roysa was afraid of the head of the family, Mr Yoyne (Jonah) Rozenblum, because he had one leg missing (at the age of eight, he had been hit by a bullet above the left knee), and she never went there again. I was not afraid of Mr Rozenblum. He was a kind and very friendly man, as well as a very clever one. His wife, Mariem (Miriam), was a warm, lively person and had a heart of gold. As time went by and I became a frequent visitor to my newly found friends, my mother became envious of Mrs Rozenblum, telling me often that I had two mothers.

There were three children in the Rozenblum family: Ruchl (Rose), born in 1920, who became my trusted and adored friend; Fishl (Felix), born in 1922, the only son; and Malke (Maria), the youngest, born in 1926, who was a beautiful girl, but very spoiled by her parents, consequent to her surviving an extremely serious illness in infancy.

In the beginning, Fishl was like a stranger to me. He was a serious boy, not very talkative, and mixed mostly with his schoolmates. When Fishl began working, at the age of fourteen, he always came home with a newspaper in his hands, reading it while he was walking. Most of the time, he seemed not to notice us, a group of teenagers who usually crowded their place and talked, argued, laughed, and sang. Fishl seldom got involved, and kept at a distance from us.

Some time in 1938, Fishl all of a sudden began to notice me. Although he never admitted it, I suspected this happened after he learned that his cousin Fishl Wajnsztok, who was in love with me, complained about my indifference. Fishl was an intelligent and interesting boy. We soon realised that we liked each other, became friends, and began to spend time together. He took me to the cinema, to theatre plays, and to concerts. After a short time, it occurred to me that Fishl was in love with me. My feelings were similar. It was not long before we became sweethearts.

While still at school, I was once approached by a teacher of my younger brother, Dovid, asking me if I would like to tutor some boys who had difficulties learning the Polish language. I gladly accepted the offer, and made some pocket money, too.

The same year, a girlfriend asked me if I could help out during the school holidays, finishing knitted garments. They would teach me to sew buttons, make buttonholes, and attach collars by hand. I said I would give it a try. My girlfriend's parents lived in a two-room apartment with their four daughters. During daytime, their bedroom was converted into a workroom. I worked there during all my school holidays and for some time after I finished school. I spent all the money I earned on clothing for myself and for my young sister, Bayle.

I had hated Poland since I was a child. My greatest desire was to emigrate to another country one day, to leave behind the blatant anti-Semitism and the poor living conditions of my country of birth. Some years ago, while I was attending Adult Education English classes, I wrote this short essay about my childhood:

> To describe my childhood is like describing a long unpleasant journey in a strange country. Unfortunately, I was never fond of the place I was born. I think that it is not enough for a child to be loved by his or her own family. A child, like an adult, needs a sense of belonging to the country and to the fellow-citizens.

I am Jewish, and I was born in Poland. I lived with my parents, two brothers, and sister in a Jewish quarter of Lodz. Outside our quarter, Jews were often physically attacked. I was always terrified of the hatred shown towards us by some young Polish larrikins. As a young girl, I once witnessed a pogrom, an event which I will never forget. I saw poor, defenceless Jews being beaten up in the street and in their apartments. I heard women and children cry. I saw old men lying in the street in agony and I can still remember their pale faces, trembling with fear, unable to understand why they were attacked.

I wished and dreamed that I could fly away to a far-away country, where there was no hatred and people lived in harmony with their fellow-citizens. Years went by, my dream was fulfilled, but something is missing in my life, a very important part in the development of every person — a happy childhood.

Chapter Two

WHEN THE war broke out, in 1939, I could not comprehend what had happened, could not make any sense out of it. I was only sixteen years old. Suddenly I found myself living under German occupation. All Jews, including my father, lost their livelihoods. Then, in April 1940, the whole Jewish population was herded into a ghetto, as in medieval times. Over 200,000 were squeezed into a few square kilometres in the poorest, dirtiest part of the Old City and Bałuty (where we already lived). Most of them were dispossessed, without work, without food. I grew up quickly to understand the enormity of the tragedy.

Fishl did not trust the Germans from the first day of their arrival in our city. As their brutality towards Jews mounted from day to day, he feared that the situation of the Jewish people in Poland, especially the young men among them, would deteriorate dramatically. On 21 November 1939, Fishl fled Lodz, with the consent of his parents, and went to the eastern Polish territories, occupied by the Soviet Union. It was a very sad day for his family and for myself. His parents worried a lot about how he would cope with the difficulties of everyday life in those uncertain times. Not one day went by when they did not mention Fishl, their beloved, only son. His mother had tears in her eyes whenever she spoke about him.

I knew that Fishl's parents loved me, but his departure brought us closer together. Immediately after his departure, they asked my mother's permission for me to stay with them for a week. Fulfilling his mother's wish, I slept in Fishl's bed during the whole week I was with them. I left the ghetto in April 1941. Before I left, there were occasions when Fishl's mother insisted that I take a portion of her bread ration, and practically forced me to eat it on the spot.

I wrote regularly to the Rozenblums from Unterdiessen, my first labour camp in Germany. Once, I received a parcel from them containing summer dresses, shoes, and a beautiful scarf: it was a special gift from Fishl's father. I was envied by every girl in the camp. In the end, I had to cut the scarf in two and give away one half to a friend. Fishl was in the Soviet Union and I was in Germany — a world apart — with a slim chance of us seeing each other again. However, that did not stop Fishl's parents from caring for me. I loved them and respected them, hoping to show them my gratitude one day. Unfortunately, their lives were cut short — they perished in the gas ovens of Auschwitz in August 1944.

The first summer in the ghetto was bad enough. Then came the winter. There was not yet any organised food or ration distribution. People — especially the elderly — starved to death or died of cold. Bread queues stretched for miles. Soup kitchens were the main supply of nourishment. But to obtain a bowl of soup one had to line up from early morning until late in the day.

My family suffered terribly. They believed that God was with them and would not let them down. I was the oldest, and my brothers and sister looked to me for an example; but I just lay in bed, starving and crying all the time. I was not pushy enough for the bread queues, and too proud to stand all day in line for a bowl of soup. I was disappointed with life, depressed, and very weak.

When spring arrived at last, there was an announcement that young women were being sought to work in German labour camps. I enlisted as soon as possible. Of 1,500 women registered, only sixty-eight were accepted. I was the last one. My parents agreed that I should enlist. They knew that I would not survive in the ghetto. I was too proud; I was not tough enough for it. In Germany, they thought, I might have a slim chance.

A few days later, in April 1941, I took leave of my family and went to the assembly point for the departure to Germany. The most difficult one to part with was my young sister, Bayle. She loved me so much. She was eleven years old at the time, and was very dear to me.

The first labour camp they brought us to was Unterdiessen, in Bavaria. They housed us in three wooden barracks, surrounded by a barbed-wire fence, and we were sent out to work in the fields of a large flax enterprise. It was very hard work for us, city girls who were not used to such labour. Our hands bled, and all our bones ached after a long day in the field.

We were not given enough food; however, we were better off there than in the ghetto. Nevertheless, it was a sad life. We were not allowed to go out of the compound or to have any contact with the outside world. We entertained ourselves by celebrating each girl's birthday; we wrote cards and poems. I used to do a lot of the latter to occupy my mind. We also read books.

In the autumn, we were transferred to Buchloe, to work in a factory that processed raw flax. We stayed there all winter. In the spring of 1942, they sent us to Lohhof, near Munich, where we did the same work as in Underdiessen. Later in 1942, our whole group of sixty-eight was sent to an ammunition factory in Augsburg. There we were employed in the production of very small weapons' parts. They taught us to operate machines and to use magnifying glasses and tweezers. They called us by our proper names — 'Fräulein this' or 'Fräulein that' — instead of by the first names we had been called in other camps. The German supervising engineers were the first people in Germany to treat us like human beings.

Although it was strictly forbidden to have any contact with us, one incident is worth noting. A German worker quietly approached us and told us that he, his wife, and son would like to help us. He suggested that he and his young son could mend our worn shoes, and his wife would try to get for us articles of hygiene, which we needed very much. Every day, we left a parcel of a few pairs of worn shoes at an arranged spot, and he picked it up, mended the shoes at night, and delivered them to the same spot the next day. We also got the articles of hygiene from him, which his wife bought for us. All of us were very grateful to those noble Germans. They kept helping us until we left Augsburg. As a token of gratitude, we gave them a signed picture of our whole group, taken in a previous camp. To my great surprise, that picture appeared in a book of war memoirs in the 1950s, with a caption: 'A group of 68 Jewish girls, sent away from Augsburg in 1943, to an unknown destination.' The picture could only have been obtained from that German family.

In the spring of 1943, the policy of the Nazis changed: they set about making Germany *Judenrein* — that is, cleansed of all Jews. They gave each of us a ration of bread and marmalade, told us to pack our meagre belongings, and put us on a train, ostensibly going to a labour camp in Poland. While we were being searched before our departure, one official told me to throw away my many small items of a sentimental nature — my friends' birthday greetings and letters — and to replace them in my suitcase with food. There was, however, no food available. Two days later, we arrived at a railway station marked Auschwitz.

Chapter Three

THE FIRST THING they did was to take away all my possessions, and tattoo in ink a number with a triangle on my left forearm. Each time the needle went into my skin, it drew blood. It seemed to take such a long time. I cried all the time, but I still did not know what was ahead of me. This was only the beginning; we were so ignorant. We had no idea what was happening to us, because we had never heard of this place before.

Then they shaved off my hair completely. I cried so much. I had such beautiful hair. At that time it was fashionable to have ringlets like Shirley Temple's, and when they shaved off my hair I became numb. With every cut, I died a little. Everything inside me died. From that moment on, I felt that I was not alive anymore, because my mother had always been so proud of my hair. My mother always used to tell me: 'Oh, you're beautiful.' When the Germans invaded Poland, her only worry was that they might cut off my hair. That was her biggest worry. She did not suspect that something worse could happen to me.

I will never forget the beginning of that madness. I felt:

This is the end. Something is very wrong.

Afterwards, we had to stand completely naked in a queue, and a woman started to shave off my pubic hair. German SS men with machine-guns were standing around us and watching. I was told to stand with my legs wide apart to make her job easier. I was an innocent girl. No man had seen me naked before.

Then they sent us for a shower in a big building. After the shower, we had to get some clothes. Ours had been taken away by the female inmates who were in charge of us. There was a huge table with clothing on it, from which I was handed a Russian soldier's uniform that felt as though it had come from the First World War. After I put it on, somebody painted a large cross on my front and back. They also gave me a scarf to put on, but my bare head could not hold anything; it was too slippery.

When I went out, I caught a look at my face in the reflection of a window. I thought: *This is Hell. This is impossible. What is happening here cannot happen in a real world among normal people. How could normal people do things like this to other people?* It did not make sense. I could not understand. Why did they do this to me? What for?

I thought: *The one who arrived here is dead. This is not me. From now on, I am not the same. I am a different person, and I don't know what they want from me.* I wanted to die. I said to myself: *I'm still alive. I'm dead and alive.* I did not know whether I was more alive or more dead. I was thinking: *How can I walk? How can I look at myself? The best thing for me would be to drop dead. Just to drop dead.* That was my wish.

Afterwards, they kept us in quarantine for six weeks. When it ended, we sixty-eight girls, who had been together for so long, were separated and sent to different barracks. I was assigned to *Ausser-Kommando 104* (outside work outfit 104). We were led to work by armed SS men with large dogs. We were made to carry heavy rocks from one place to another. The hard labour was of no use to anybody; its only aim was to inflict pain and humiliation, to torment us. On the way to and from the camp, we saw the smoking crematoria chimneys. We understood. This was where all of us would end up. The German guards jokingly told us that it was the *Himmel-Kommando* (the heavens' work outfit).*

The daily routine of terrible hunger, cold, exhaustion, overcrowding, and lack of the most basic means of personal hygiene, coupled with cruel beatings, soon reduced the number of able-bodied inmates considerably. To make things worse, an epidemic of typhoid fever raged in the camp. In the late autumn, I, too, succumbed to the epidemic.

A lot of people were sick. They were taken to the so-called sick bay, an empty barracks with no doctors, no medications, without anything to help the sick. There were just a number of orderlies doing their best — which did not amount to much. The sick were cramped on the bunks, as in the other barracks.

---

* Auschwitz I had a gas chamber and crematorium, but was mainly a forced-labour camp, unlike the death-camp Birkenau (Auschwitz II), which was three kilometres from Auschwitz I. Fela's assignment to the *Ausser-Kommando*, and her subsequent reference to Dr Mengele, whose role overseeing selections happened at Birkenau, points to her being at Birkenau rather than Auschwitz I.

They put me beside a girl who had diarrhoea. I could feel her wet, soiled legs. She had a high temperature, and so had I. Once a day, they came around with some food — a piece of bread and some watery-coloured stuff called tea. I covered my head and refused to take it. I said: 'I am not hungry, I do not want to live.' I was not sorry for myself; I was quite happy. I thought: *Now is probably the end of my suffering, and I'm glad it will soon be over*. I had lost my will to live. I was sure that I could not survive in those surroundings. It was just a matter of time.

In the sick bay, selections were an everyday occurrence. When a selection was on, everybody had to be down from their bunk and on their feet. The SS men would walk through the barracks and assess each inmate. The inmates whose numbers were written down were sent to the gas chambers. The people who did not come down from their bunks were automatically sent to the gas chambers.

A few days after I was admitted to the sick bay, a selection took place. I did not come down from the bunk. Some people were afraid to show their forearms. They wanted to live. In those terrible conditions, sick and miserable, treated worse than animals, they still wanted to live. If they could, they would hide in the tiniest nook or cranny, just to escape being sent to death, just to stay alive a little longer.

It was a large barracks, housing about 1,000 sick women. I was lying semi-conscious and happy in the knowledge that I would not suffer much longer. That evening, somebody woke me up. It was Fela Hamer, a girl from our original group of sixty-eight. She was a nursing aide in the sick bay, and she had spotted me by pure accident.

She said: 'Fela, is that you? I can't believe it. You have been put on the list for the gas chambers. You are too young to die. I must save you.' I begged her to leave me, to let me go. I kept on repeating: 'Please let me die.' Another girl from our group, who was lying nearby, overheard us and started to yell at Fela: 'Please save me, I want to live, she doesn't want to, please save my life.' Fela told her that she could only save one, and she wanted to save me. To this very day, the desperate voice of that girl rings in my ears.

The notorious Dr Mengele was at that time in charge of the selections. Fela went to him, and told him that I was her sister and the only one left in her family. She begged him not to send me to the gas chambers. Although he was not such a noble person, Mengele granted her wish because Fela was respected by the Germans for being a very good worker. Maybe it was pure luck that, when Fela approached him, the usually beastly doctor was in a good mood.

I had been having a dream when Fela Hamer woke me up. My body felt as light as a feather, and I was moving upwards, higher and higher. I felt no pain at all. I heard a horrible noise, like the wheels of a passing express train, and through it a loud voice calling my name: 'Fela Perelman, Fela Perelman' (my maiden name). When I woke up at Fela Hamer's urging, I heard a nursing aide say: 'This one will not survive the night. In the morning we will have a corpse.'

That following night was the night of the crisis. Without medication, lying beside a diarrhoea sufferer, I survived. But to survive the crisis was not enough. I was still sick with typhoid; I was still so weak. The problem was, how could I survive the next selection and not be sent to the gas chambers? In normal times, when one has typhoid fever, one goes to a hospital, has medical attention, is on a proper diet, is cared for, and has the affection of one's family and friends. I was alone, without help, worse than an animal. Nobody cared about me, except my girlfriend, Fela Hamer. To me, she was like an angel. What she did for me was the only normal thing in that mad world with mad people called Auschwitz. She took me into her quarters and gave me some food, but I had no appetite.

The next day, before the trucks came to pick up the sick people marked for the gas chambers, Fela gave me a nurse's uniform to put on. She forced me to get up, because it was dangerous to stay on the bunk. I could not walk, so she made me lean on her back. When the SS men made a rollcall, I stood behind her, and nobody could see that I was so sick. She washed me, dressed me, and did everything else that was needed.

As sick as I was, I had to do some work because I was supposed to be a nursing aide. I had to help my friend get the sick people onto the trucks — the trucks that were taking them to the gas chambers. What an irony! I was meant to be one of them. I was too weak to be of any help.

I was given a chance to survive, but I needed the physical strength to carry out some nursing duties. There were no toilets in the barracks. To relieve themselves, people used large buckets, one in each corner. I was asked to carry the buckets to a special truck, a fair distance away. It was winter, snow was falling, and the ground was slippery as I went out carrying a heavy bucket. I walked step by step, frightened that I might slip. While carrying the heavy bucket, I had to cross over a deep gutter. I had no strength at all. I put the bucket on the ground first, then lifted one knee with both my arms, and then the other knee. To empty the bucket into the truck I had to lift it up on a ladder. In the days to come, this was the job I had to do a few times daily.

When I recovered sufficiently and was fit enough, Fela told me that it would be better for me to go back to the camp. She saved my life, and I regained my will to live.

Our friendship was to last until her death in 1992. We met again in Lodz, after the end of the war. She was just getting married to Laybl Herszberg, and I was present at their wedding. In the following year, in 1946, I married Fishl, after he returned from the Soviet Union, where he had survived the war. Fela and her husband organised our wedding, and gave us away. We had no immediate family. They acted as our parents, as brothers, as sisters.

In 1947, the Herszbergs and their first-born son left Poland and went to Australia, settling in Sydney. At the end of 1951, after living in Paris for nearly five years, we too migrated to Australia, but chose Melbourne as our home. We visited the Herszbergs, who became very religious, in Sydney; and they came to visit us in Melbourne on many occasions. Unfortunately, Laybl Herszberg died some years ago. Fela remarried and lived with her husband in Israel until her sudden death in October 1992. We corresponded frequently, and Fela used to come to Melbourne every few years to visit some of her very large family.

Chapter Four

THE PEOPLE who knew me before I got sick were very surprised when I came back to the camp. They were sure I had been dead for a long time. Not many people survived typhoid fever in Auschwitz. That must have been in the first months of 1944. I felt physically stronger, and began to adjust to the everyday bleak and cruel life of an ordinary inmate of the concentration camp.

During the spring and early summer, transports of Jews from different towns in Europe kept arriving practically every day. The horrible process of the annihilation of defenceless people was in full swing. After disembarking, the new arrivals faced their first selection. All children, older and handicapped people, as well as anyone who looked emaciated, were sent to their final destinations. In August 1944, transports from Lodz, my hometown, began to arrive in Auschwitz. The whole population of about 70,000, from the last ghetto in Poland, was sent to Auschwitz in railway cattle-trucks, packed like sardines.

Next to our barracks was an empty lot. One day, about 800 females from a Lodz transport were herded together in that lot. Any contact with them was strictly forbidden.

Somebody told me that my best girlfriend and her younger sister (both sisters of my future husband, Fishl) were among the new arrivals. Since I had come to Auschwitz, I had never expected to see them again. That evening, after I received my bread ration and the so-called tea, which was my whole sustenance until the next evening, I decided that I had to try to see them. I did not hesitate for a moment. I knew that they would have had no rations, perhaps for the last few days.

I went over to the new transport and moved among the people, clutching the bread and tea. There was a terrible chaos among the women: some of them cried, others screamed incessantly. At last, I found my girlfriend and her sister. I gave them my bread ration, but the tea was spilled by the hands and arms of people who desperately wanted a drink. I left them quickly, but on the way back to my barracks I had the misfortune to be caught by the German SS woman in charge of the whole women's camp.

She grabbed my shoulders and hit my head against a brick wall until I was semi-conscious. I am sure she would have killed me if it was not for our barracks kapo, a Czechoslovak girl, who had observed the whole incident from the window of our barracks. She rushed towards me, grabbed me from the German woman, and hit me very hard on both sides of my face. Sure that she had left me in good hands, the German SS woman left, handing me over to the barracks kapo to finish me off. However, to my great surprise, the Czechoslovak girl led me to the barracks and went away without uttering a word. I did not feel any physical pain, but my suppressed emotions got the better of me and I cried hysterically for a long time.

The gas chambers and crematoria could not keep up with the large transports of Jews arriving every day from Hungary and from Lodz. There simply was no room for such huge numbers of people. Those who passed the first selection were kept in the camp only for a short time — some of them just a few days — then they were put on trains and sent to different camps in Germany or occupied countries.

Life in Auschwitz dragged on. Towards December, rumours began to spread that the Russian army was approaching, and that the whole camp would be evacuated. We noticed that the German SS were wearing civilian clothing under their uniforms. They wanted to be ready to shed their SS uniforms in case they were caught by the Russians. Then they began to burn documents from the camp offices. They lit fires, and tried to destroy the evidence of their horrible crimes.

When we were told officially that we would be leaving Auschwitz, we could not believe it. We all thought that not one of us would survive that horrible place, that hell on earth. Because we were not only the victims, but also the living witnesses of what had happened there, we assumed that the Germans would not allow us to survive.

We were to leave Auschwitz, but among us were too many sick and weak people of all ages. Myself, I was in a terrible condition. I had diarrhoea and I had nothing to wear, except a blanket and wooden clogs. Then my guardian angel, Fela Hamer, found me and gave me a bundle of clothes and some bread, which I could not eat — I was too ill. Fela looked so well and healthy. I was more on the delicate side. There was usually something wrong with me, but I was lucky; people always wanted to help me.

Before we set out on foot from Auschwitz, in the middle of winter, there was chaos, complete anarchy in the camp. Strong women broke into the kitchen and grabbed all the food they could find. Our destination was Ravensbrück. We marched on country roads, five abreast. The stronger people were always in front. The weaker ones lagged behind. We walked day and night. Armed SS men and women walked with us. Anyone who fell on the road and could not march on was shot on the spot. We were walking over corpses all the time. It was called the death march. We walked for days and nights, and lost count of time and distance.[*]

From time to time, a command was given for a short rest. I was always at the back of the column. When the command to rest reached us, it was already time to get up, and I never had a rest. I was so weakened by the diarrhoea that I often thought: *I will not go on. When they command me to get up I will not, I will just sit down and let them shoot me.* Each time I had those thoughts, I heard a strong voice telling me: 'Get up, go, go.' Later I met Fredzia Diament, a girlfriend from our original group of sixty-eight. She was in the company of

---

[*] The death march to Ravensbrück, north of Berlin and the largest women's concentration camp, started in mid-January 1945. The distance covered was at least 600 kilometres.

another girl I did not know. We were happy to have met again, and my spirits rose in their company. Somehow the walking became easier, too. As for the things Fela had given me, they were too heavy for me to carry. I threw them away, little by little.

When we arrived at Ravensbrück, the camp was grossly overcrowded. Nothing was as organised as in Auschwitz. There we were always under the threat of going to the gas chambers; but when the time arrived, you got your ration of bread and so-called tea. If there were 800 inmates, there were 800 portions; if there were 200, there were 200 portions. In Ravensbrück, there was nothing. The whole place was in chaos. There was nobody to take care of us.

When we came into a barracks, there were sick people everywhere. There were bunks like in Auschwitz, but most people were lying on the ground. If one wanted to get up on a bunk, one had to tread on those on the ground, mostly sick ones. No one would tell you: 'Here is a place for you.' Everything was mixed up. It was sheer bedlam. To get a ration of bread, we had to stand in a queue outside. When we came back to the barracks, we had no bunk; somebody had taken away our planks. We were tired and hungry, and had nowhere to sleep.

Next day, when we went to pick up our rations, I said to my friends: 'One of us should stay and guard our newly acquired planks, and we will share our ration with her. We will have less to eat, but we will have a place to sleep.' So one of us stayed behind, but afterwards everyone was hungry and miserable. We had so little food that it was impossible to make do with less. The next day, I suggested to the girls something funny but very practical: 'Each of us should take a few planks when we queue for our rations.' It worked well. We could save our planks and have our full rations.

On one occasion, we were queuing for soup but were told there was no more. The whole barrel of soup had been taken away by a group of strong Ukrainian peasant women. They had stolen the food allotted to a few hundred people, and gorged themselves on it for three days. They did it in full view of hundreds of hungry people, who watched them doing it but could not take any action against them. Those women were too strong; they could kill you if you started an argument with them.

Because Ravensbrück lacked any sort of organisation, we had so little food that we could not survive. One day, a German arrived and picked 500 girls to go to a labour camp in eastern Germany. I, as well as a few other girls from our original group of sixty-eight, was among those 500. That was in the spring of 1945, a time when every one of us had a feeling that the war was going to end soon. Whatever lay ahead of us could not be as bad as Ravensbrück, and we hoped that we would survive. Besides, if we had come out of Auschwitz alive, everything was possible.

It was not so bad in that labour camp. There were no German armed guards. They were trying to save their own skins. Soon afterwards, they told us they had to evacuate us, and we became frightened. We did not trust them; how could we? They assured us that they would not harm us, but did not tell us that the war was nearly over. They convinced us, and we went with them. The Germans told us that the Russians were not far away and that they were leading us towards the American army instead.

When we stopped for a rest in a forest, I and two other girls decided to leave our guardians and hide. We heard their whistles and their commands to get up, but we hid behind a large log. We were in a huge forest. Later we met a lot of Poles, German deserters, and runaways from different camps hiding there. The Germans were unshaven, dirty, looked miserable, and were frightened of the advancing Russian army. We stayed in the forest for the next twenty-four hours. For the first time, after all those years of imprisonment, we felt free.

In the morning, we left the forest and went to a nearby farm. They gave us some bread and milk, and advised us which direction we should follow away from the forest, which we felt was not safe for us. We found an abandoned farmhouse, where a large Polish family had worked for the previous German owners and had stayed on. We decided to stay on with them. The previous owners, rich farmers, had left in a great hurry. The front line was very near, and we had to share an underground bunker with the Poles during frequent bombardments. When the bombardments stopped, we stayed on that farm. We had no radio, and the farmhouse was so isolated that we did not know how the war was going. Some time later, we met a group of passing Russian soldiers. They told us that the war had ended two weeks before, on the eighth of May.

Chapter Five

THE WAR HAD ENDED, but my misery was far from over. I was alone in the whole world. What I had witnessed and experienced in Auschwitz and in Ravensbrück had made me suspicious of the human race. I trusted no one. Like a newborn baby, I needed a lot of love and affection to begin a new life.

In the chaotic post-war situation, I came back to Lodz in June 1945. Despite my sad memories of the city of my birth, I had to return there for two reasons. Firstly, I wanted to see if anyone in my family had survived. Secondly, Fishl and I had promised each other to meet in Lodz if we survived the war. I went to 21 Młynarska (Mill) Street, where we used to live, hoping to find a familiar face there. There was nothing there — the whole building had disappeared. There was only grass on the site, like on a cemetery but without graves. I then crossed the street and knocked at the door of the apartment where Fishl's family used to live. A Polish woman opened the door, but refused to let me in. I had to accept the terrible fact that no one from my family had survived. As for Fishl, there was no news of him yet. My only hope was that he was safe and well in the Soviet Union, and that he would come back soon.

I was very naive, thinking that the Poles would be more compassionate towards us after what we had gone through during the war years and the wholesale slaughter of Polish Jews. It was unbelievable, how hostile and anti-Semitic they still were. I heard many Poles complain: 'So bloody many of them survived.' I could not believe my own ears.

Accommodation and work was scarce in post-war Lodz. Through an acquaintance, I found a temporary apartment in the Polish quarter of the city, and I lived there with a girlfriend. The owner of the premises was away on business and did not use his apartment. He was a man of about forty. In my eyes, however, he was an old man. After a few months, he came back and proposed to me. Despite his generosity, I could not marry him. I began to look for other accommodation.

Back in June, as I was walking on the street, I met a friend from Auschwitz, Ala, who was originally from Warsaw. She had married just before the war, and was still young and attractive. She was overjoyed to see me, and invited me to a café. As soon as I told her that I needed a job, she said: 'Fela, I've got a job for you.' She was working as a cashier in a well-known Jewish restaurant, and promised me that she would tell her boss how absolutely honest I was. She was sure that he would employ me.

When Ala mentioned my honesty, I saw in front of me the block in Auschwitz where we had been together. She worked as a nurse and, as such, was not under the threat of being sent to the gas chambers, as most of us were. I worked in the *Weberei* (weaving room), situated far away from our block. We produced ammunition containers, made up of small pieces of leather, which we had to cut and stretch. It was a very difficult and dirty job. There were 400 of us working there.

One day, my friend Ala asked me to deliver a love letter to a Pole who was the chief cook for the German guards. When I delivered her letter to him, he sent her in return a container of cooked food. I never even looked inside the container before delivering it to my friend. Considering how hungry I was at the time, Ala was very impressed by me. I had my reward when she gave me some of the food. For quite some time afterwards, I was her regular carrier.

What I was doing was very dangerous. Before passing the camp-gate entrance with the sign *'Arbeit macht frei'* (work liberates you), we were often searched. The German kapos were looking for cigarettes, valuables, and other forbidden items. For carrying a love letter, I risked a punishment of twenty-five lashes on my bare bottom. One morning, while I was carrying a letter, there was a search on, at the gate. A kapo spotted me from far away — I was probably behaving suspiciously while throwing away the letter. She searched me and found six cigarettes. She said nothing, but hit me very hard on the face with both her fists, and left me. My face was sore, and I was crying; but, according to other girls in the group, I was very lucky. She pocketed the cigarettes. If I had had only one or two cigarettes, she would not have bothered to take them, but would have reported me immediately, and I would have been given twenty-five lashes — a horrible experience, from which the victim could suffer for many years.

How did I come to be in possession of six cigarettes? For each letter delivered to the Polish cook, I received a cigarette from him, which in the camp had the value of a daily bread-ration. I could exchange a cigarette for bread anytime. At that time, there were rumours that the inmates from our block would be moved to another part of Auschwitz. I did not know what to expect, and had saved the cigarettes for a time of greater need. Losing the cigarettes put an end to all my careful plans.

Ala was right. Her boss received me well and offered me the job. After suffering hunger for so many years, being deprived of the most essential food, such as milk, butter, eggs, cheese, fish, meat, and vegetables — not to mention fruit — the restaurant was, for me, and for the other people working there, a virtual paradise. We could choose to eat anything we liked. For breakfast, lunch, and dinner, as well as supper, we had the most tasty and nourishing food there was. True, we had to work long hours, from 8.00 a.m. until 11.00 p.m. It is also true that we did not earn much money, because the cost of our food was deducted from the wages. However, it was still a terrific place to work for the personnel of twelve.

I replaced a salesgirl who got married and left. I worked in the front hall of the building, leading to the main restaurant. We sold delicious takeaway food. As well, there were tables and chairs for food to be consumed on the spot by people in a hurry. People could order *gefilte* (stuffed) fish, roasted brisket, or anything they desired. They could take away boxes of chocolate, all sorts of bread rolls, sausages, etc. Apart from the food being consumed there, the restaurant was also a mirror of the post-war Jewish population. The place was always full of people, talking, rushing, and looking for familiar faces, just like at a railway station.

While working at the restaurant, I put on a lot of weight. As compensation for the wartime years of deprivation, when I was continuously undernourished and very skinny, I ate everything, not worrying about becoming fat. I and another girl worked there as salesgirls. Ala, my friend, was the cashier, and there was also a barmaid, called Sonia. After Ala left Poland, some time later, Sonia's sister Gucia took over the job of cashier. Sonia and Gucia are still alive and live in Melbourne. We see each other from time to time.

By sheer chance, I met on the street a cousin of Fishl, Szmulek Rozenblum, whom I had got to know at Fishl's parents' place before I had left for Germany. This was probably at the end of June. Szmulek told me that there was a postcard from Fishl, mailed in Siberia, on the noticeboard of the Jewish Community Centre, inquiring about his parents, his sisters, and me.

From the moment I learned that Fishl was alive in the Soviet Union, a wonderful, jubilant feeling entered my whole being. The news that he had survived and was inquiring about me seemed just like a fairy tale. I wrote to him immediately, but it took two months for the letter to reach him in Siberia. Waiting for a reply from him seemed like an eternity to me. I was in a perpetual trance.

In my loneliness, I remembered Fishl as the person who could bring me back to a life I was longing for. At that time, I had heard of many cases where young couples, who had become separated during the war but survived, did not get in touch with each other afterwards, for different reasons. A number of people were amazed then, and for years to come, that Fishl and I had retained our longing for each other during such a long separation, in different corners of the world — they looked at us and kept wondering.

After the war, I had many marriage proposals. I refused them all, mostly because I was afraid of people and did not trust them. I was still a virgin, and intended to remain so until my wedding day. I made up my mind not to sell myself just for a roof over my head or some other material gains. I was determined to work hard and not to give in. While working in the restaurant, I was surrounded by many newlywed couples. I was horrified to see how badly matched they were. In most cases, the men were much older than the women. I felt very sorry for them, and understood the circumstances that had forced them into those marriages.

My young life had been interrupted by the cruel and barbaric war. I felt that a part of it was missing. I needed love and true friendship to bring me back to life. True, I had not seen Fishl for six years, and he might have changed. Sometimes those thoughts came to my mind, but I trusted him. The way I remembered him, he was honest and good — and I loved him.

After many months of waiting, I received a letter from Fishl. It was full of love and tenderness. He begged me to be patient and to wait for him, because he still did not know when he would be able to come back to Lodz. In the weeks to come, I sometimes received three letters at the same time. The postman once made a joke: 'So many letters at the one time prove that you have not slept with him yet.' At that time, I was already living with Szmulek Rozenblum and his wife, Hanka, at 59 Piłsudskiego Street.

I met Szmulek one day on the street, and I told him that I had to move out from where I lived, and I asked him if he could help me with accommodation. He understood my problem and, with his wife's permission, I moved into their apartment. They put a bed for me in a corner of their bedroom and treated me like a sister. I became very friendly with them, particularly with Hanka. I appreciated very much what they did for me, and shared the living expenses, paying one-third of the bills.

At that time, the restaurant had already closed. Thanks to Fela Hamer, her husband gave me a job in his factory. He taught me to operate a power yarn-spinning machine. It was all piecework, and I became very quick and efficient at the job. Sometimes, Hanka used to bring me breakfast to the factory, because the young couple liked to sleep in, and I did not feel like having breakfast by myself. Hanka was a wonderful girl. She was pretty, and very much in love with Szmulek. She had lost her parents in the Lodz ghetto, at the age of twelve. Szmulek was her distant cousin. They both were among the 800 people who had survived within the ghetto, and they got married right after the end of the war.

As time went on, letters from Fishl arrived nearly every day. His departure from the Soviet Union was approaching, but I was still uncertain of the exact date. Early in the morning of 19 April 1946, as I was getting ready to go to work, I heard a knock at the door. I opened the door, and there was Fishl — standing there and smiling at me. He was in the company of a stranger, whom he later introduced as his old army friend with whom he had come back from Siberia.

I was pleasantly surprised by how well Fishl looked. The boy I remembered was no more. He looked manly and handsome. We embraced with tears in our eyes. The reality was too fantastic to believe in. After a while, I introduced Szmulek Rozenblum and Hanka to Fishl. I did not go to work that morning. All day we did not stop talking and rejoicing over the memorable event of being united at last.

That first night, in Szmulek and Hanka's bedroom, will stay in my memory all my life. We lay in each other's arms whispering. I told Fishl about Auschwitz, about the gas chambers, and about how Fela Hamer had saved my life. We both wept, and spent a sleepless night (and so probably did the other Rozenblums). Because of our excitement and emotion, we lost our appetite for food in the following weeks. Despite having been separated for six-and-a-half years, despite having been so far away from each other, and despite the dangerous and horrible times we had gone through, our destiny had been fulfilled. Miraculously, we had survived and met again. Soon, we would be married and would begin a new life together.

PART TWO

Felix

Preface

In April 1992, on the eve of my 70th birthday, my son Henry came to our place one day and dropped a small Macintosh computer on my desk, saying: 'Now, Dad, you'll have no more excuses. You'll have to write your memoirs.' As soon as he installed the computer, he began instructing me how to use it, promising to spend as much time with me as necessary until I became fully familiar with it.

For a number of years, both my sons, Henry and John, had been nagging me to write down my life story. They did not agree with my attitude — that I had survived the war years in the comparative safety of the then Soviet Union, and that only people who were incarcerated in ghettos or concentration camps or had been in hiding from the Nazis should leave eyewitness accounts of those terrible years

My sons insisted that I owed it to them and to their children to write down the story of my childhood and early youth in Lodz; how I survived the war-years in the Soviet Union; and, most importantly, the miracle of meeting my sweetheart, Fela, after the war ended; our subsequent wedding; our departure from Poland; our nearly five-year stay in Paris; and, finally, our emigration to Australia.

I had no option — I could not find any more excuses for delaying writing. I rolled up my sleeves and sat down to write my memoirs. It is my sincere hope that these memoirs will justify the expectations of those who prodded me to write them.

Chapter One

MY FATHER, Avrum Yoyne (Abraham Jonah) Rozenblum, was born in 1897, in the small town of Sulejów, in central Poland, then a part of the Russian Empire. He was the last of the six surviving children of Yitta and Avrum Yoyne. When he was born, my father was already fatherless. His father, aged thirty-five, had been critically injured during a fire in their bakery a few months earlier, and had died soon after. So, in accordance with Jewish tradition, the newly born son was named after his father.

At thirty-three, the widow Yitta, my grandmother, was left with six children: five boys and one girl. Unable to support them in Sulejów, she moved to the large city of Lodz, at the request of the brothers of her deceased husband. The boys were sent to work as soon as it was possible. At the age of twelve, Yidl (Julius), the eldest, was already a qualified baker, a trade he had learned from his father. The other boys — Yekhiel (Harry), born in 1887; Mendl (Morris), born in 1889; and Maniel (Max), born in 1892 — would start tailoring apprenticeships as soon as they reached the required age. Their only sister, Aydl, was born in 1896.

In 1905, when my father was nearly eight years old, a revolution started in St Petersburg, and soon spread to other parts of the vast empire. Strikes, large public demonstrations, and meetings became a daily occurrence. Lodz, an industrial city with well-organised, although illegal, trade unions and political parties of the left, was one of the centres of revolutionary activity.*

The Russian police and military, stationed in the city, were very brutal in their attempts to quell any public dissent. They used whips and sabres, and very often shot at unarmed civilians taking part in the illegal gatherings. The most feared among the military were the horse-riding Cossacks, from the Don steppes. They were vicious, merciless, and often sadistic in their actions to uphold law and order.

One morning, as my father, perhaps imprudently, was on his way home from *cheder*, a primary-level religious school for boys, some demonstrators were being chased by Cossacks. One of the Cossacks took aim at the frightened, running boy, and for sheer fun pulled the trigger.

The bullet hit my father above the left knee, came out, and struck the right foot. Some bystanders took the bleeding boy to a nearby doctor, who in turn had the boy transported to a hospital. Father's life was saved, but his left leg was amputated above the knee. For the remainder of his life, father would walk with the help of two crutches.

---

* The revolution broke out in January 1905, but disturbances in Lodz only reached their peak in June.

His four brothers and their only sister eventually left Poland and migrated to the USA. Yekhiel went first, in 1907, followed by Yidl, who was by then already married and had a small child. Maniel went in 1910. Mendl and Aydl waited one more year and travelled together in 1911. Because the immigration laws of the USA forbade the entry of people with any physical or mental disability, grandmother Yitta knew that her youngest son, my father, would not be allowed to join them. She was determined to stay with him, at least until he was an adult.

They remained in Lodz, where grandmother, who had remarried, had another son, Laybl (Leonard), born in 1909. After the end of World War I, at the age of twenty-two, my father married Mariem (Miriam), my mother. Only then did grandmother heed the continuous pleas of her children in the USA, and begin to plan her departure.

She left at the end of 1922, and she took Leonard with her, the son of her second marriage. At that time, my father was already well settled in family life and had two children — the first-born, my sister Ruchl, born in 1920, and myself, six months old. Until she died, in 1944, grandmother had a soft spot for her crippled son, left behind in Poland. Until the outbreak of World War II, she wrote to him often and sent him gifts of money on every Jewish holiday.

My mother was born in Sandomierz, a historic town in southern Poland, where the river San falls into the Wisła (Vistula). She was the youngest child of Fishl Mayer and

Kayle Ruchl Kruk.** Grandfather Fishl was a furrier by trade. In 1902, he decided to move with his family to Lodz, a rapidly growing industrial city. There were five children in the family: the oldest, Nakhe, born in the late 1870s; Perl, born in 1879; Mordkhe, born in 1885; Yankl, born in 1887; and my mother, Mariem, born in 1890. In all probability, grandfather did not do too well, financially, in Lodz. However, all the children got married in the big city.

As a matter of fact, the elder daughters, Nakhe and Perl, were married on the same day, in 1903. A few years later, Mordkhe found a bride; and Yankl married not long before World War I began, in August 1914.

The Russian imperial army was soon driven out of Lodz by the advancing German troops, which were to occupy the city until Armistice Day, 11 November 1918. During the years of the German occupation, the civil population suffered severe hunger. The Germans looted the country of all the foodstuffs they could lay their hands on, and left very little to feed the population.

Grandmother Ruchl died in 1914. Grandfather Fishl followed her in 1916. Both died of malnutrition. To save herself from starvation, my mother, at the age of twenty-five, enlisted for road-building works for the German army. Her brother Yankl was conscripted by the Germans for forced labour in a chemical factory in Germany. He never came back to his wife and two very young daughters. He died there

---

** Kayle Ruchl was the second wife of Fishl Mayer Kruk. His first wife, Chana Priwa Hajblum, died young, apparently without having had any children.

of poisoning, near the end of the war. Mother's two sisters and their families barely survived. The only one who did a little better was her brother Mordkhe, who was a good tradesman cobbler.

After the armistice, mother returned to Lodz, which by that time was the second-largest city of the newly independent Polish republic. She was twenty-nine, an orphan, and quite poor. It was probably through a matchmaker that she met her future husband, my father. He liked her immediately. Grandmother Yitta gave her blessing to the marriage, which took place in 1919.

Grandmother's intuition proved right. The young couple were in love from the day they met. They always respected each other. She considered him the wisest and best man in the world. He thought that he was lucky to have her for a wife. Although father had received only the usual Jewish religious education, he later taught himself to write and read Yiddish, as well as Polish. He became a voracious reader and, little by little, abandoned religious practice, except for going to the synagogue on the High Holidays and continuing the traditional Friday-evening welcome of the Sabbath.

Despite his physical handicap, father was always a good provider for his family. After his hosiery manufacturing set-up failed, he became a stallholder at a market, selling men's clothing. When times were tough, during the Great Depression of 1929–1936, mother successfully helped out to earn a living. We, their children, grew up in a home full of love and kindness. The first-born, in 1920, was named after grandmother Kayle Ruchl (Rose). I was born in 1922, and named Fishl Mayer (Felix), after grandfather. My younger sister was born in 1926 and named Fraydl Malke (Maria) after grandmother Yitta's mother. We had the best parents one could wish for.

In August 1944, both of them arrived in Auschwitz from the Lodz ghetto, where they and my two sisters had survived for four-and-a-half years. According to an eyewitness, mother looked fit, and easily passed the first selection. She was directed towards the camp, but she consciously clung to her beloved husband and walked with him to the gas chambers, where they died together. Without him, life had no purpose or value for her.

Chapter Two

MY EARLIEST MEMORY of my mother is walking with her in the street, in summer, munching a piece of bread. I was probably four years old. Mother met some of her friends and stopped. As they engaged in a conversation, I suddenly began to choke on a piece of crust. I tried to attract mother's attention by pulling her hand and pulling her skirt — all to no avail. She kept on talking to the ladies. In desperation, I kicked her in the leg. Only then did she realise my predicament. She gave me a few solid slaps on the back, and I was saved.

My sister Malke is four years younger than me. When she was nearly one, she contracted meningitis and was critically ill. During her illness, my older sister, Ruchl, and I stayed with our two aunties, who lived together in a large but run-down apartment, about one kilometre away.

One day, our aunties came with us to visit our parents. We were not allowed to enter our one-room apartment, and instead talked to our parents through a small opening in the door. There was practically no furniture in the room — only a bed, on which my little sister lay, a table, and one chair.

Both my parents were crying, and asked us to leave, which we did in a great hurry. Much later, I learned that we had come on the day of crisis for my sister. She was only one breath away from death, but by some miracle pulled through and survived, with no apparent damage. When I was older, I understood that all the furniture had had to be sold to pay for the doctors and medicines.

As soon as I reached the age of five, mother, who came from a religious home, enrolled me in a *cheder*. One day — it must have been in the summer — a group of us were sitting around the table, prayer books in front of us. It was late afternoon, and I felt very hot in the small, stuffy room. Suddenly, I saw my father through the window, beckoning me to come out. I excused myself and went out to him. He embraced me, told me the weather was too hot to stay inside and study, then bought me an ice-cream in a nearby shop. We sat there for a while, then went home together. When we were in the courtyard, father winked at me and said: 'We will tell mother that you were sent home earlier today, because of the heat, and I met you on the street.' I loved him for that little conspiracy.

In September 1928, at the age of six, I went to school for the first time. It was a secular Yiddish primary school, where my sister Ruchl was already in the second grade.

The winter of 1928–1929 was one of the coldest on record. Transportation was at a standstill, coal was impossible to get, and people were freezing. Schools were closed, and we stayed home, dressed in the warmest clothes mother could find.

One morning, our father left early, telling us that he had been promised a cart-load of coal if he could pick it up personally at the railway yard. It must have had something to do with him being an invalid. The three of us, and mother, stood at the window waiting for father. Then he appeared at the entrance gate of the court, walking beside a horse-drawn cart full of coal.

When he entered the courtyard, the cart was suddenly encircled by a great number of people, the tenants of the building. They were desperate. Normally peaceful and friendly neighbours, each of them grabbed as much coal from the cart as they could. Father's pleading and shouting did not help much. He was left with very little of the precious coal.

Father was very angry for a while. Then he sat silently for some time, got up, and told us that he was not mad at our neighbours anymore; they were simply desperate, and needed the coal, just as we did.

One Friday, early in the spring of 1929, the principal of our school called me out of the classroom and asked me to fetch mother right away. We lived about 500 metres from the school. Excited, I ran all the way home and conveyed to my mother the message from the principal. Intrigued by the urgency, she followed me to the school and went to see him. What he wanted was my mother's permission to promote me to the second grade for the remainder of the school year.

Apparently I was scholastically advanced, well above the level of the other kids in grade one, and the teachers had recommended that I should jump a grade in mid-year. On the following Monday, I was presented to the children of grade two by my teacher. I was only six years old. At the end of the school year, at the age of seven, I was promoted to grade three. Most of the other students were already nine years old. For the remainder of my school years, adolescence, and even later, I would always associate with people who were a couple of years older than myself.

Our school belonged to the CJSZO (Central Yiddish School Organisation), founded in 1921, under the influence of the Jewish Socialist Party, the Bund, and it adopted the standardised Yiddish spelling of the YIVO, the Jewish Institute for Scientific Research. The CJSZO schools were the only ones in Poland where all subjects, except Polish language and literature, were taught in our mother-tongue, Yiddish.

The majority of our teachers were young, idealistic, radical people, who set themselves the goal of bringing modern, secular education to Jewish children. They were particularly zealous in their love for Yiddish, and considered the upgrading of its status and tuition methods as their sacred duty. Despite being poorly paid and overworked, our teachers infected us with their enthusiasm and love of education. They encouraged our quest for learning and knowledge, and gave each student individual attention. At a time when corporal punishment was the norm in most schools, it was unknown in ours.

I loved the school and its teachers, and was very happy there. I had good friends, and enjoyed the camaraderie of students and teachers. Learning came easily to me. In consequence, I was good at most subjects, especially maths. The principal, who was our maths teacher, proudly called me her 'little mathematician'. I was also a voracious reader. Soon the school library was inadequate for me. On the suggestion of the teachers, I began to borrow books from the large Grosser Library, which was situated at least three kilometres away from where we lived. But I did not mind. As a matter of fact, I enjoyed my visits to the library very much.

The atmosphere of our school was like that of an extended family. It was our second home. The students were close to each other during their school years, and remained very good friends after graduation. The classmates kept in close contact even after the terrible years of the Holocaust. The survivors, spread over different countries and continents, have retained to this day their warm, fraternal feelings. We have written to each other over the years and met whenever possible. Such meetings have always been very joyous occasions. The close bonds, cemented at our school, were to last forever.

When I was eight, in 1930, I became seriously ill with scarlet fever. At that time, it was a much-dreaded, highly infectious children's disease. A doctor was called, and he gave me an injection in the lower left abdomen. To this day, I can still remember how painful it was. However, it must have been very effective. I started to get better quickly, but no one, especially children, were allowed to visit me.

Every afternoon, after school, my classmates assembled in the courtyard, below our second-storey apartment, and yelled out in turn, to share with me the day's happenings at school. I appreciated very much their thoughtful expressions of friendship, and recovered quickly to join them at school.

In 1931, my parents decided that our apartment at 17 Młynarska Street, where they had lived since getting married, was too cramped for the family of five. They found a much larger vacant apartment about 160 metres away, at 14 Berek Joselewicz Street (so named after a famous Jewish participant in a Polish uprising against Russia). We moved to the new place, which was on the ground floor, in the far corner of a huge courtyard, on the opposite side of which were stables for horses and the equipment of some teamsters who lived in our building.

One particular summer evening, our whole family came home from some sort of celebration. Father, who had had a few drinks, was in a very good mood. We sat outside our apartment enjoying the lovely evening. Then we heard the coughing of our upstairs neighbour, a young woman in her early twenties, who was suffering from consumption. Father's mood changed immediately, as he told us tearfully: 'That poor girl will not last much longer — what a pity, what a waste.'

His prophecy proved to be correct. She died a few weeks later.

We did not stay very long in the new apartment. There was dampness on most of the walls, and my parents were very concerned that this could affect the health of their children, especially my sister Ruchl, who was more delicate than the other two. In 1933, after an absence of less than two years, we moved back to Młynarska Street — though to the other side, to number twenty.

That was a nice brick building. However, it had only a small courtyard. Our apartment was on the first floor facing the street and had a balcony, which my mother soon filled with flower boxes and plants. She loved gardening, and was very good at it, too. All our relatives and visitors had to inspect her balcony as she proudly showed them each flower or plant. Mother had what is called 'green fingers', and she always had larger and prettier flowers than anybody else.

From the first day, our family was happy in that apartment. It was always full of young people — our schoolmates and, later, after leaving school, my and my sisters' friends. Both our parents were on very friendly terms with the young people. They never complained of the noise we probably made on many occasions. They were happy to see us in the company of so many youngsters: arguing, singing, dancing, or just being in the company of friends.

In that apartment, I met my Faygele (Fela) for the first time. It was probably in 1934, when she came to see my sister Ruchl, with whom she became friendly. In that apartment, our family lived through the terrible years of the Nazi occupation in the Lodz ghetto until the bitter end, the liquidation of the ghetto.

As I have mentioned before, our school was under the influence of the Jewish Socialist Party, the Bund. As soon as we got a little older, we were actively encouraged by the teachers to join Skif, their children's organisation. I, in company with most of my classmates, became a member of Skif when I was about ten. That was the beginning of a new and very interesting period in my life. The organisation was divided into groups of about twenty. Each group had a leader, an adult — in most cases, a teacher from our school — and sent one of its members as a representative to the council, which ran the whole organisation. The group leader or a guest speaker held weekly talks about current social and political events. We also had outings, summer camps, and participated in all Bundist festivities.

I enjoyed the camaraderie of my fellow Skifists, and became very interested in the theoretical teachings of the founders of socialism. At the age of twelve, I read the works of Marx, Engels, Bebel, and others. I was voted to represent my group, and became a member of the council. I even managed to write an essay under the title 'Socialism and Women', based on the writings of August Bebel, and I read it at a special function of Skif. Within a short time, I was convinced that socialism would solve all the problems and ills of the Jewish people and of the entire world. I considered myself a fully fledged participant in the struggle for socialism.

Religion was not taught at our school. The seeds of anti-religiousness were firmly planted in our minds. At Skif, religion and religious practices were treated with contempt and disdain. It went so far that on Yom Kippur, the holiest day of the Jewish calendar, we would be busy helping to make a success of the party's special press-day. We ran around the Jewish quarter selling the daily newspaper of the Bund, the *Naye Folkstsaytung*, completely unaware that we were badly hurting the feelings of tens of thousands of people who were walking to or from the synagogues.

Before Passover 1934, the principal of our school, Mrs Liza Holtzman, had a talk with me and three other boys in our class. Since that was our final year at the school, she proposed that for the last three months of the school year we should attend a government Jewish primary school, the principal of which was a lifelong friend of hers.* Her idea was that we would get a graduation certificate from that school in order to increase the chances for any one of us who wanted to continue his education to receive a bursary to a government high school. She feared that the authorities were biased against our school because the subjects, except Polish and Polish literature, were taught in Yiddish. She then asked each of us to call a parent to see her immediately, to get their approval.

It was again on a Friday, as it had been five years before, when I told my mother that the principal wanted to see her.

---

* Under the provisions of a treaty agreed at the Paris Peace Conference in 1919, the newly restored Polish state was obliged to fund public elementary schooling for its national minorities, and to protect minority religious freedoms. The treaty was always controversial in Poland, which renounced it in 1934. A treaty provision requiring teaching at minority public schools to be in minority languages (such as Yiddish for Jews) was never implemented.

This time, though, I was able to explain the reason. Mother was very excited and happy. She knew that I was doing well at school, but had not expected such a development. She went to school with me and gave her approval without consulting father. That same afternoon, Mrs Holtzman accompanied the four of us to meet our new principal and to enrol us in the new school.

Naturally, we were nervous. But the principal, Mr Shelubsky, welcomed us cordially and quickly put us at ease. He seemed to be very friendly with our Mrs Holtzman. Like her, he was an old revolutionary, an intellectual, a gifted and hard-working educator, who had come to Poland from Russia after the October Revolution.

Mr Shelubsky was right. We had nothing to fear. Our educational standard was higher than that of our new classmates. Although only two of us, my friend Avrum (Alan) Wolf and myself, had been top students in our previous school, even the other two, considered average, did very well in the new school. We all graduated with high marks in June 1934. I was only twelve.

Some time later, a decision had to be made about my future because the government had rejected my application for a bursary. We held a family conference, and I was told by my parents that, if I wanted to continue my education, they would be prepared to pay the necessary private high-school fees. My answer was that I could not place such a heavy financial burden on the whole family, especially in those times of economic hardship. I told them that I would wait until I could begin an apprenticeship in a trade, when I turned fourteen. In the meantime I could become a tutor for slow-learning children in our school. In fact, I had already made inquiries and had been promised a few tutorials. My parents reluctantly accepted my decision.

I began tutoring as soon as the school year started. The pay was pitifully low, but I enjoyed it. I gave my mother all the money that I earned, and I was the proudest person in the world when, some time later, father went with me to buy cloth for a new suit. Then he found a tailor, who made up a suit for me. It was the first time in my life that I had paid for something myself, with the fruit of my own labour.

It was a tradition in our family to prepare our own Passover wine. Usually this was done immediately after Chanukah, in December. Mother and father went to the market and brought home a box of grapes, usually a little damaged and therefore cheaper. Then mother would wash them, allow us to help to press out the juice, add some sugar, and put it away to ferment in a very large glass bottle. The filtration of the fermented juice was a job that mother did not entrust to anybody — she considered herself an expert in that field.

It was a tedious and time-consuming job. A special grey cardboard funnel was made and filled with charcoal, and put in the throat of another, similar bottle. The liquid had to pass through it very slowly, drop by drop. Father rigged up a special stand for the top bottle to keep it nearly horizontal. Mother kept on saying that the secret of good wine was slow filtration, repeated as many times as possible.

That winter, when I was twelve and had already finished

school, father woke me up one night, gave me a sign to be silent, and asked me very quietly: 'Would you like to taste the wine — just to see how it is coming along?' That was the first of many tastings. From that year onwards, mother would wonder why she lost so much wine in the distillation process. However, when Passover came there was usually plenty of wine left.

Chapter Three

SINCE I HAD FINISHED primary school and had not gone on to further education, I was not sure what trade I would like to learn. As I was approaching my fourteenth birthday, I had to make a decision. I chose printing, which was wholeheartedly approved of by my parents. My father found an employer willing to take me on as an apprentice compositor. After Passover 1936, I began my career in the printing trade — a trade in which I stayed until my retirement.

The apprenticeship was for a duration of three years. The starting pay was very low, but would be raised at the beginning of each following year. Despite the long working hours (46 hours per week), I liked the workplace, and got on well with the employer, the tradesmen, and the other people. I was very interested in learning as much as I could in the shortest time possible. Two months after I started work, the Jewish Printing Employees' Union called a strike of all its members. Although apprentices were officially exempt, I, being a fully convinced socialist and union member, enthusiastically joined my workmates in their industrial action. This was my initiation into the class struggle — the practical expression of socialist theory.

Every day I went to the union premises, which were full of people. I listened to the speeches and heated discussions between the leadership and striking members. My first great disappointment in the validity of the theory of the international solidarity of the proletariat came very soon. The Polish Union of Printing Employees refused to join us in the struggle for better pay and conditions. They found some hollow excuses, but the simple truth was that they did not want to co-operate with Jews. As a result of their action, all printing firms (mostly non-Jewish) that employed their members could fill all the available printing orders in the town, to the detriment of Jewish employers who were handicapped by the strike.

The strike folded after a month without achieving any gains. The fear of substantial job losses among its members convinced the union leadership to give up the fight. Until the beginning of World War II, there was not another strike of Jewish printing workers in Lodz.

Yom Kippur, the Day of Atonement, is the holiest day of the Jewish calendar. Most Jewish people in pre-war Poland, religious or non-practising, observed it. Mother would always fast from sunset of the preceding day until sunset of Yom Kippur. In the morning, she and father went to the synagogue for the whole day to pray. Mother knew that we, I and my sisters, would not fast, and made sure that there was plenty of food left in the house. When we sat down to the traditional evening meal, after our parents came home from the synagogue, mother never asked us how we had spent the day. She respected our ways, but she herself could never depart from maintaining the traditions with which she grew up, nor her basic religious beliefs.

Father was different. As we grew up, we could detect a continuing change in his attitudes towards religion. In fact, he attended synagogue services during holidays just to please mother. Although he had received the usual religious education during his childhood and youth, including some time at a *yeshivah*, he became disenchanted with religious practice as he got older. He read a lot, and I believe he was sympathetic to the ideological approach of our school on the subject of religion and my developing strong commitment to socialism.

On Yom Kippur in 1938, father and mother left home, as usual, in the morning and went to the synagogue. I left before them, since that was a special promotion day of the Bundist daily. At lunchtime, after we had finished selling the papers, I went with a group of friends to a nearby eating place. On that holy day, we took a special revenge on God. We had the great pleasure not just of breaking the law of fasting, but we indulged ourselves by eating Polish-cooked pork sausage and sauerkraut.

After the meal, in the mid-afternoon, I and a few friends decided to see a film in the nearby cinema. At that time, the screening was continuous — one could come in the middle of a film, and then there would be an interval and the next screening would start. We bought our tickets and were ushered to our seats in the darkness. When the interval started, I was very surprised to find my father sitting in a row behind me. Father leaned over and told me in a whisper that he had sneaked out of the synagogue because he was bored and could not take it anymore. Under his arm, he had a neatly wrapped package that held his prayer book and shawl. With a conspiratorial wink, father told me not to mention a word about our meeting to mother.

He left the cinema soon after and went back to the synagogue, just in time for the start of the evening service. After sunset, father and mother came home from the synagogue together. They were in a very good mood. Mother and sister set the table for the traditional meal to break the Yom Kippur fast. At the first opportunity, father gave me a wink and went on to recite the kiddush (the blessing for wine recited at the start of most Jewish ritual meals).

Adolf Hitler became Reich Chancellor of Germany in 1933. As a direct consequence of that event, the political and economic situation of the Jewish population began to deteriorate steadily. The poisonous anti-Semitism of the German Nazis spread like an epidemic across eastern Europe and found very fertile ground in Poland. Government restrictions on trade, employment, and education for the Jewish population became commonplace. The universities restricted the enrolment of young Jews through the imposition of a strict quota system. Jewish students were forced to sit in the back rows at lectures and tutorials, and were often beaten up by their fellow Polish students.

The Jewish middle class was hit by an economic boycott, publicly called for by the anti-Semitic political parties and quietly approved of by the government. Jewish workers were denied employment at any government-funded bodies or in non-Jewish-owned enterprises. Even Jewish-owned larger enterprises were forced to restrict the number of Jews they employed. Outbursts of physical violence against Jews were an everyday occurrence. This culminated in a large pogrom in the town of Przytyk, near Kielce, in March 1936, when a Jewish couple was killed and a large number of Jews were injured by a mob of looters.

The police stood by and did nothing until young Jews started to defend themselves and one of the attackers was killed. Arrests were made, and a couple of months later a trial was held of more than thirty peasants and a dozen Jews. According to the prosecutor, the Jews had attacked the peaceful peasants and were responsible for the pogrom. Most of the peasants were freed. Those who had murdered the Jewish couple were sentenced to a few months' imprisonment. The Jewish accused were sentenced to several years of hard labour.

The Polish government stated openly that there were at least one million too many Jews in Poland and that they wanted them to leave as soon as possible. The problem was that there was nowhere for them to go — the whole world had closed its doors. The ill-winds of the approaching storm were blowing stronger and stronger. Between 1933 and 1938, fascism was advancing across Europe and elsewhere. Abyssinia (Ethiopia), Spain, Austria, the Sudetenland — they were all conquered, yet the beast was still not satisfied and demanded a lot more.

We, the politically aware young people, still believed in the brotherhood of man, in the international solidarity of the workers, in socialism. We believed and hoped that the unthinkable would not happen.

For years, Fela had been a frequent visitor of my sisters' in our apartment. She was a shy, good-looking, and likeable girl with a contagious laugh. She became a close friend of my sister, and she mixed well with all the young people who usually came to our place. I always thought that my parents had a soft spot for Fela.

It was not until the middle of 1938 that I began to take notice of Fela. It did not take me very long to realise that I wanted to be in her company and to go out with her. This was not very easy, since she had very religious parents who would strongly disapprove of their daughter meeting with a young man. To overcome that problem, Fela and I had to work out a special, secret arrangement. Whenever we wanted to go out, Fela would leave home in the company of my sister or another girlfriend, then meet me in the city at a pre-arranged spot. On our way home, we usually separated some distance away from the street where we both lived. Fela would return to her place alone, and I would go home a little later.

In those times, I was very lucky to receive complimentary tickets to concerts and to theatres. Our firm had a contract to produce bill posters for the entertainment industry. It was customary for the senior apprentice to deliver proofs of the posters to the clients. Usually they checked them, made some alterations if necessary, and gave the apprentice two free tickets to the advertised event. That was quite a bonus. I can still remember taking Fela to the Philharmonic Hall, to a recital of Joseph Schmidt, the famous Austrian tenor; and to the State Theatre, where they usually presented plays of very high quality.

In the summer of 1938, we went to a sports festival and open-air concert organised by the Bund-sponsored *Kultur Lige* (Culture League), in Lodz's Helenów park. Fela came to the park with her friends, and I came with my friends, but we managed to be alone for some time. As the year 1938 drew to a close, the whole group decided to celebrate New Year's Eve. We went to a ball and had a very good time. I danced with Fela all night. A heavy snow was falling when we went home in the early hours of the morning. As we approached our street, I stayed behind as my sister accompanied Fela to her place.

In the new year, my feelings towards Fela deepened. True, we were both very young. Nevertheless, it was genuine love — the first and only love in my life. I considered her my sweetheart, and I had reason to believe that my feelings were reciprocated by Fela. In the months to come, those feelings grew stronger and stronger.

In April 1939, I finished my apprenticeship. Despite the fact that I had first-class references from my employer, I could not find a job as a compositor in any printing firm in town.

The economic and political situation at the time was so uncertain that employers were unwilling to hire additional labour. I was very disappointed, because I wanted to further my experience in the trade in new surroundings. When my employer proposed that I stay on working for him, I reluctantly accepted his offer.

Spring 1939. A war seemed imminent. Hitler made very heavy territorial demands on Poland: annexation of the corridor between Prussia and East Prussia; full sovereignty over the free city of Danzig; and other adjustments to the Polish-German border. The government of Poland declared that it would not cede one inch of its territory, and ordered a partial mobilisation of its army. The Jewish population of Poland, although treated as second-class citizens, proclaimed their readiness to fulfil their duty in the defence of Poland against Nazi Germany.

England and France, which had previously signed formal military agreements with Poland, realised that their policy of appeasement towards Germany could not be continued. They realised that if it came to war they would have to stand by Poland in her hour of need. Feverish diplomatic activity went on through that beautiful summer of 1939. Then, like a bolt from the sky, on 23 August, came news of the signing of a non-aggression pact between Nazi Germany and the Soviet Union.

The two hitherto bitter enemies had joined forces and signed an additional secret protocol that was only revealed after the war: it allowed them once again to partition Poland

and give the Soviet Union a free hand to annex the Baltic States, parts of Romania, and a slice of Finland. As well, the two partners signed an elaborate trade agreement. The Soviet Union became the principal supplier of strategic raw materials to Nazi Germany. Hitler, assured of Soviet neutrality to the east, was now ready to unleash his military might on Poland, despite the obvious risk of forcing England and France to fulfil their obligation of coming to her assistance.

Chapter Four

FRIDAY, 1 SEPTEMBER. The mobilisation of all militarily trained men was proceeding at a furious pace. In the previous week, all able-bodied people were asked to help dig anti-tank defences around the city. Thousand of citizens responded to the call. The government-run radio and newspapers kept up their patriotic fervour, claiming that 'Poland will not surrender even one button of a military uniform to the Germans.'

In the morning, as I was getting ready for the day's work, the street below us suddenly filled with people. The radio and the early-edition newspapers announced that the dreaded war had started. The German armed forces had breached the border at many points during the night, and were encountering fierce resistance from the Polish army. The civilian populations of many Polish cities were under aerial attack from the German air force. The first air alert sounded soon afterwards. The unthinkable had happened. World War II had begun.

Sunday, 3 September. Despite the obviously deteriorating situation at the front and in the mercilessly bombarded cities,

Poland and its citizens hoped for a swift reply from their allies, Great Britain and France. There was jubilation in the streets and in the homes when Great Britain and France declared themselves at war with Germany later that morning. The radio kept repeating the joyous message: 'England and France are with us, victory is assured now.'

Despite those assurances, the brisk advances of the mighty German war machine could not be stopped by the badly led, ill-equipped, and inadequately trained Polish army. Even the most gallant cavalry in the world was no match for modern tanks and armoured vehicles. Not one English or French aeroplane appeared over Poland to challenge the might of the Luftwaffe, which dominated the skies. Although battles were still raging in a number of key points, the main defence line in the west of the country was virtually crumbling. Unable to withstand the onslaught of the mighty German forces, a large number of disorganised Polish army units were retreating towards Warsaw, to defend the capital city. All roads leading to Warsaw were already clogged with the military as well as with thousands of civilians, fleeing from the advancing Germans.

In the afternoon of Tuesday, 5 September, the government radio announced a strategic retreat of all military units from the Lodz region. The same announcement urged all able-bodied males, between the ages of eighteen and forty-five, to leave the city during the night and to head towards Warsaw, to help defend the capital. Panic broke out as rumours spread that Lodz had been virtually abandoned by the military and government officials. Fearing air attacks in the daylight, tens of thousands of men left their homes during the evening, and joined the masses of people and vehicles on the overcrowded roads.

I had to make a decision. True, I wasn't yet eighteen, but I thought I had a moral obligation to help defend the capital against the Germans. I explained the situation to my parents, who respected my point of view. I filled a small rucksack with a few necessities and a little food, and left home. The road was full of people, and we moved very slowly. After five hours, we reached the small township of Brzeziny, a distance of only twenty-four kilometres. It became even harder to walk. Some people began to turn back. Daybreak was not too far away. Soon it would be too dangerous to stay on the road. I hesitated for a while, then decided that I could not go on. I had to hurry back to Lodz.

The German army marched into Lodz on Friday, 8 September. My heart sank as I watched the units of this mighty, modern, and well-equipped army passing the arterial road leading towards Warsaw. The German soldiers looked unbeatable. No wonder the Polish army was in retreat. There were only a few pockets of resistance left, apart from Warsaw, a city under continuous bombardment from the air and virtually besieged. The heroic defence would last until the end of September.

During the first weeks of the German occupation, the Jewish population of Lodz felt like condemned people awaiting their execution. The new administration was not yet in place. Industry and commerce were at a standstill, and no one went to work. Only the bakeries and shops dealing in foodstuffs opened for brief periods during the daytime. Most people spent the days at home, in the nearby streets, or visiting friends living not too far away. Owners of radio receivers were the most sought-after sources of information. Warsaw was still defending itself against the overwhelming might of the Germans, there were still fierce battles raging in a few places, and there was still a little hope left that England and France would do something for Poland.

During those days, Fela, who lived just across the street, used to come over to us nearly every day and stay in our place a good deal of the time. Despite our grave fears and uncertainty about the future, our love grew stronger. My parents openly showed their approval of her, and treated Fela like a member of the family. My two sisters also shared my parents' feelings towards Fela.

On 17 September, the news spread that the Red Army had crossed the Polish border and was advancing from the east, towards the River Bug. The remainder of the embattled Polish army, in retreat from the German onslaught, were trapped in the part of Poland that was by then under Soviet control. They had no option but to surrender to the Soviet army. The Russians promptly dispatched all officers to POW camps. Most of the enlisted men were freed and allowed to go home.

The symbol of Polish resistance, Warsaw, under siege since the beginning of the war, still held on defiantly, waiting for help from the Allies, as they had provided once before in

August 1920, when the Soviet army reached the Vistula. Alas, England and France did not come to the rescue — in fact, they did nothing.

Devastated from the air, without power, food, or water, Warsaw, capitulated to the Germans on 27 September.

Lodz had a sizeable ethnic German community before the war. In fact, the huge textile industry of Lodz had been established and developed by Germans and Jews in the nineteenth century. Since then, the two communities had always had friendly, neighbourly relations. All that changed when the Nazis came to power in Germany. As soon as the German army marched into Lodz, these ethnic Germans, the *Volksdeutsche*, put on swastika armbands and became the guides and advisers of the new administration. They had previously prepared lists of leading socialists, communists, and active trade-union leaders. During the first week of the occupation, those people were hunted down and put into a hastily set up camp in the suburb of Radogoszcz. The victims of that round-up were never seen alive again.

A short time later, the government issued a proclamation, expropriating all Jewish real estate and industrial machinery. This was followed by an order prohibiting Jewish doctors and lawyers from practising their professions with non-Jews. News spread that army personnel, in the company of ethnic Germans, were evicting many Jewish families from better-class apartments in the centre of the city, at short notice. Then began the indiscriminate grabbing of Jews — mostly men — off the streets or even from their houses, to form work parties. Generally, the work was cleaning houses or other buildings for the new administration, and it was usually accompanied by mockery and sadistic, physical mistreatment. Especially vulnerable were the religious people. Young Nazi thugs would savagely beat them up, then pull out their beards and fringed locks, leaving their faces a bloody mess.

I was grabbed for such a work party only once. With about ten others, they led me to a private house, on the outskirts of the city. They told us to clean it well, and promised to let us go as soon as we had the job finished. I was lucky: they kept their word.

As September ended and October began, the majority of the Jewish population was without any income. Most factories, stores, and shops were still closed. The working class and the lower middle class, who had very little or no savings at all, were in great poverty. Since there were as yet no laws restricting the movement of Jews, the more adventurous ones began to travel to the countryside by any means available. Despite the obvious risks, they managed to buy or barter any available produce and bring it to the city, where they easily sold it at a profit.

Reliable eyewitness reports became available from the Soviet-occupied territories of eastern Poland. Soldiers of the Polish army, whom the Russians allowed to return home, told of masses of refugees arriving there daily from the German-occupied part of Poland. They spoke of German atrocities in towns and villages across the whole length of the border, and said that the total Jewish population of some of those places had fled to the Soviet territories. They confirmed that the larger cities such as Białystok, Lwów, Kowel, and Równe were full of refugees and that, even though accommodation was rough and pretty hard to obtain, the Jewish population there was free and happy. Of even greater importance to me were their statements that crossing the border was not too difficult.

I and most of my friends were immediately attracted to the idea of fleeing from the German occupation. I had enough political awareness not to trust the Germans. I thought that it was only a matter of time before the full severity of the Nuremberg Laws would come down on the Jews of Poland. Since they had come to power in 1933, the already manifested pathological anti-Semitism of the Nazis, their cold-blooded brutality towards the German Jews, and the openly proclaimed war against the Jewish people by their leader, Adolf Hitler, put me in no doubt of the mortal danger that all Jews who remained in Poland were in. Unlike some older people who had survived German occupation once before, during World War I, who claimed that things would settle down, I was sure that the situation would worsen. I was convinced that anyone who was able to should flee to eastern Poland, while they still could do so.

Towards the end of October, news spread that some people had returned from German captivity, and that they were in very bad shape. Among the arrivals was my schoolmate Avrum Wolf. I went to visit him a few days later. He was unrecognisable — terribly thin, still sick, and very weak after his long ordeal. His first words to me were: 'Run, Felix, run, do not stay here. As soon as I am well enough to travel, I'll leave, too.' He told me how he had been captured by the Germans not far from Warsaw during that ill-fated march from Lodz, at the beginning of September, and how he and about 1,000 other Jewish prisoners were kept in the open for three days without food or water. They were put into railway cattle trucks and ferried across Germany, like caged animals, unshaven, often beaten up, getting very little food or water, and forced to do the most debasing tasks. They were photographed at every railway station, as examples of the sub-human Jews. Finally, they arrived at Cracow, where the Jewish community was forced to pay a substantial ransom for their freedom.

As soon as I came home, I suggested to my parents that our whole family should leave together. I pointed out that we were all adults, and that despite father's physical handicap we would succeed. I told them that we could start planning for our departure — sell as many of our household goods as possible, and prepare ourselves for the journey. I added that if they were not willing to leave, I would like their permission to go by myself, or with a friend.

My parents were not ready to leave their home and to travel into the unknown. They dreaded being uprooted and among masses of refugees. Father then asked me to reconsider my request. He thought that the family should stay together, for the time being at least. I had to wait.

In the second week of November, a Jew and two non-Jews were publicly hanged in the Bałuty market-square

— allegedly for being thieves and black marketeers, but nobody believed that explanation. We suspected that it was done to arouse fear and to terrorise the Jewish population. Then, a few days later, an order appeared, giving effect to one that had been issued a week earlier: from 21 November, all Jews would be required to wear a yellow armband, 10 centimetres across, to make them more recognisable on the streets. The announcement listed the death penalty for not conforming to the order.*

That evening, after dinner, my father told me that he had changed his mind and would not oppose my departure from Lodz. He said that although he had always believed that a family should stay together, in good times as well as in hard times, the present extraordinary circumstances had made him reconsider his views. The future looked very uncertain, and we should be prepared for the worst. Men, especially the young ones, might be in the greatest danger. He had come to the conclusion that he did not want to have it on his conscience that he had stopped me from saving myself, when it was still possible.

He added that, should I decide to leave, he would help me with anything he could. He advised me that, since I was only seventeen, it would be better for me to find a travelling companion. Perhaps my first cousin, Fishl Wajnsztok, who was three years older than me, would like to go with me.

---

* This was the first time in any area under Nazi rule that Jews had been required to wear distinctive clothing. On 11 December, after Fishl had left, the order was amended to require a yellow Star of David on the chest and back.

When father finished, he had tears in his eyes. The five of us around the table wept uncontrollably for some time.

I contacted my cousin, and he immediately agreed to join me, but confided that he had no money at all, and could not get any from his poor parents. My father promised to raise enough cash for both of us. We decided to leave on 21 November, the day the armband law was to come into force. The Germans announced that penalties for non-compliance would begin on the following day, so we would not have to wear them while we travelled. We began to prepare for the journey. The weather was deteriorating, and father thought that a three-quarter heavy jacket would be more comfortable for travelling than my overcoat. He found a tailor, who made up a jacket for me in a few days. Mother got me a rucksack, and filled it with all the necessities.

Our destination was Białystok, in the Soviet-controlled zone in eastern Poland, and the plan was quite simple. We would go by tram to the railway station and catch a train to Warsaw. From there, we would take a train to the town of Małkin and walk to the border, a few kilometres away. Of course, we would have to elude the military patrols on both sides of the border, but we were told that this was not too difficult. Father volunteered to get us the train tickets. He reasoned that it was safer for him to move around, because he was an invalid — the Germans would be less likely to grab him for work duties or abuse him physically.

The day of my departure approached. Leaving my family behind was hard enough for me. Saying goodbye to my sweetheart, Fela, was even harder. Many couples, older than us, solved such a problem by hastily getting married and leaving together as husband and wife. In our case, that was not an option. We were both definitely too young to contemplate it.** The day before my departure, I was alone with Fela for a while in our apartment. We both knew that we loved each other. We both knew that the future was very uncertain. We comforted each other and made a promise that, whatever happened, should we survive, we would meet in Lodz after the end of the war.

I remember the evening of our departure very well. My cousin arrived early in the afternoon. My parents, my sisters, and Fela were in the apartment. Our possessions were checked again by my parents, and they gave us last-minute instructions. We had to leave at dusk to take the tram and arrive at the railway station before the evening curfew. I hugged and embraced each of them. No one cried. We left in a hurry. I never saw my parents again.

** According to family lore, Fishl asked Fela to leave with him, but she felt unable to desert her family.

Chapter Five

THE RAILWAY STATION was full of German army personnel and police. We followed a group of people who looked like they were heading towards our destination, and quietly squeezed into an overcrowded train carriage standing at the platform marked 'Warsaw'. Not a word was spoken until the train started to move. Everyone was relieved, and people began conversations in a whisper. The trip was uneventful, and we arrived at Warsaw Main railway station in the middle of the night. There were a lot of German soldiers around and we did not feel very comfortable, but we had to spend the night there since we could not proceed until the curfew was lifted in the morning.

Our luck held, and no one bothered us. In the morning, about ten of us got onto a horse-drawn carriage, driven by a Pole who knew his business well. For a hefty fare, he got us across the city, over the Vistula pontoon bridge, which was guarded by German soldiers whom he bribed, to the Warsaw East railway station in the suburb of Praga. I had never been in Warsaw before the war, but it was known as a pleasant, large city, with lots of stately buildings and many parks. On that drive through Warsaw on the morning of 22 November 1939, I saw a city in ruins. The merciless four-week bombardment from the air and land during the September war had reduced Warsaw to a wasteland of building debris.

The station was packed with people, but we got our tickets in time to catch the train to Małkin. By that time we had had some travelling experience and were a little more relaxed. In our compartment, half of the passengers were Jews who were fleeing the Germans, and the other half were Polish smugglers who had sold their merchandise in Warsaw and were now going back for new supplies.

One of the Poles started a conversation with me. He asked me a few questions, then offered some advice. He told me that the German border police were waiting at the Małkin railway station for each train arriving from Warsaw. As soon as people got off the train, they were forcing all Jewish passengers into a separate area, subjecting them to random, savage beatings, then robbing them of their possessions. He said that, to avoid the danger, I and my cousin should jump off the train before it came to a standstill at the station, and quickly move in the direction of the border, which he described to us and then made a drawing of. He seemed to be an honest person, and wished us good luck.

We decided to follow the advice of the friendly Pole. We jumped off the slow-moving train near the station, and headed for the border. After a brisk march, in company with other people who had the same idea, we were stopped by a German border patrol, who checked our identities and allowed us to continue. It seemed that the German authorities were only too happy to get rid of as many Jews as possible. We were in 'no man's land', the narrow strip of land between the two new borders.

The area was full of people, refugees like us, huddled together in an open paddock without any shelter from the cold November evening. There were whole families, couples, and single people, from different parts of Poland, all of them waiting for the Russians to open the border and let them continue their journey eastwards. Some of the people had arrived at the border four days before, just after it was opened by the Russians for a short time, then closed again. They and all later arrivals had been waiting since then for the border to open.

I did not like the idea of just waiting, not knowing how long it might be. My cousin thought the same. We still had the crude map of the border region given to us by the friendly Pole on the train. We made a decision to try our luck by finding a way through the border. In the middle of the night, lit by a full moon, we made our move.

We began to run towards a certain point of the border. Soon we realised that we were not alone; other people were running beside us. Mounted Soviet border guards appeared from nowhere, shouting 'Get back, get back', and catching some of the people. We kept on running until we were stopped by a man who told us there was no need to run — we were on the Russian side already. He also gave us directions to the nearby railway station. We congratulated each other and rested for a while. In the morning, we had to fight our way through a mass of people on an open railway platform to get onto a train that would take us to Białystok. It was 23 November, less than two days after we had left Lodz.

Before the war, Białystok had been a medium-sized city with a population of about 100,000, half of it Jewish. Now, the constant arrival of refugees, mostly Jews from the German-occupied part of Poland, had more than doubled the number of its inhabitants. The place was shockingly overcrowded. All private accommodation had been snapped up by people who had arrived earlier. The synagogues, communal halls, and institutions were taken over by the later arrivals. When we arrived in Białystok, accommodation of any sort was simply not available in the city.

We were told that a large number of holiday cottages in Ogrodniczki, about ten kilometres from town, had been requisitioned to accommodate refugees. We had no other option, so we went there, and we were allocated a room to share with two other single men. The only furniture in the room was four straw-filled mattresses on the floor. However, we had a roof over our heads, and we were to receive a daily ration of bread, boiled water, and one hot meal.

The first week or so, I felt euphoric. It was great to be free, not to fear the German police, military, or the *Volksdeutsche* anymore. I met a few schoolmates and friends in Ogrodniczki and in Białystok. The main topic of conversation was how quickly one could enlist for work inside the Soviet Union. The government wanted to shift the mass of refugees in a hurry, but their bureaucracy was not very efficient. Registration for work in different cities of the

Soviet Union was too slow. Most people wanted to work in their trade, but, in the majority of cases, that was simply not possible when we arrived. Only building tradesmen such as carpenters, plumbers, or electricians, as well as metal toolmakers, were being sought.

My cousin and I were very eager to enlist. We had been idle since the beginning of September and we wanted to work, to be able to earn a living and get away from the handouts and the cramped living conditions. The weather was deteriorating, and winter was not too far away. We walked to the city nearly every day to enquire about available work inside the Soviet Union. By the middle of December, registrations had ceased completely. Then there was an announcement that able-bodied single males and married couples without children could register for work in the coalmines of Kizel, in the Urals, on a one-year contract.

We were desperate. We knew that it would be hard work physically, as well as dangerous, but nothing else was available, and we had no patience left to wait for something better. We registered and signed the contracts. Our departure date was fixed for 23 December.

We only had a couple of days to prepare for the trip, which could take up to two weeks. I also had to say goodbye to two of my schoolmates who had decided to return to Lodz. Both of them were homesick and lonely, and said that they could not go on living without their families. One of them, Karol Dunkiel, was actually a neighbour of mine. He tried hard to convince me that I, too, should come with them. He reasoned that my parents would be heartbroken when he told them that I had decided to sign up for work in a coalmine, in the faraway Urals.

My answer was simply that my reasons for fleeing the German occupation were still as valid as when I had departed. I still hated and distrusted the Germans, and preferred any hard work, anywhere in the Soviet Union, to living under the shadow of the Nazis. I wrote a letter to my parents and explained the situation from my point of view. Karol delivered it when he went back to Lodz. Years later, when my sisters came to visit me in Paris, they told me how happy our parents were that I did not return. During the terrible years in the ghetto, they often comforted each other with the knowledge that at least their son was safe and would survive.

Karol was trapped for four years in the Lodz ghetto, followed by nine months of hell in German concentration camps, and he was liberated in Bergen-Belsen by British troops. After the war he settled in the United States, and we later met on a few occasions. My second schoolmate who went back to Lodz was not so lucky. Chaim Eisenberg, a gifted young actor, was deported from the Lodz ghetto; he perished in a German camp somewhere.

The winter of 1939–1940 was one of the coldest in memory. We travelled to Kizel in railway cattle trucks that were fitted with bunks made of raw timber. There were about forty people, both men and women, to each truck. There were no sanitary facilities apart from one large metal vessel near the door, and people had to relieve themselves in it when the train was moving. During the frequent stops at railway stations, our main task was to steal enough coal from wherever we could to keep our stove going permanently; otherwise, we would all have frozen to death. Also, we washed ourselves whenever possible, and made use of the crude station toilets. The people in charge of our train were not the most efficient, and the supply of food was very irregular. When we disembarked at Kizel, after travelling for two weeks, the temperature was minus 35 degrees Celsius. In answer to our complaint about the bitter cold, we were told that the weather had in fact improved, and that a week before it had been more than minus 50 degrees.

As our group walked from the railway station to the Joseph Stalin mine, about six kilometres away, we were disappointed by the unmade roads and timber-covered footpaths. Kizel was quite a small, backward town, and served as an administrative centre for a dozen coalmines and two metallurgical enterprises.

We were housed in a large timber hostel, close to the mine. Each room had four beds and no other furniture. One large room in the building was allocated for recreation for the whole group. The sanitary facilities were very poor; there was only one outside toilet block. In the bitterly cold nights that were to come, this was to present quite a problem for us.

A woman housekeeper was in charge of the building and responsible for order. A military man, crippled in a recent skirmish with the Japanese, presented himself as our political commissar. His job was to try to re-educate us. We were taken to the canteen for a meal, and they told us that after three days of rest we would begin work in our new profession of coalmining.

My immediate problem was that I had run out of money. In the six weeks since leaving Lodz, I had shared everything with my cousin. During the trip to Kizel, we had spent the last of what father had given me. I was not alone in that situation. Very few of the new arrivals had any money. Our commissar fixed the problem immediately. We went to the office and received an advance against our future earnings. Each of us also received ration cards for some products such as sugar, soap, meat, and sausages. We were happy. We could pay for our meals at the canteen and purchase our rations in the store.

My parents had been wrong about one thing. They thought that, being three years older, my cousin would take care of me. In fact, from the first day after we departed, the opposite was true. He simply left all the decisions to me. He could never make up his mind on any matter, except one: he felt so sexually starved that any female was good enough. On our second day in Kizel, he was missing at the evening roll-call. The housekeeper and the commissar were frantic. He was a newcomer, out on a bitterly cold night, and they feared for his safety. Volunteer searchers went out to look for him. They found him in the early hours of the morning, lying drunk under a bridge. He had been on his way home from a party at the home of a woman he had met during the day. The next day, when he was sober, he could not understand what all the fuss had been about. He knew his way home, he said; he had just been resting a little.

Signing up for Kizel had been a great mistake. In our haste to get away from Białystok, we simply did not know what we were doing. On my first day down the mine, I realised how difficult and dangerous the work was. I was attached to a team of three miners, all Tartars. We were digging a horizontal shaft, and underpinning the ceiling and walls as we progressed. There was very little mechanisation — it was all pick-and-shovel work, and very strenuous physical labour. The really frightening aspects, though, were the constant dampness, the lack of ventilation, and the always-present danger of falling rock and debris. There were no safety rules or precautions of any kind. Although I was physically fit, and I tried very hard not to lag behind my workmates, I could not keep up with them. They were all seasoned labourers who had done that sort of work all their lives.

Despite the harsh realities of life in the Soviet Union, I wanted to learn the Russian language as quickly as possible. I thought that, after our contract was fulfilled, I would work at my trade, or perhaps continue my education and go to university. When the wife of a mine engineer, a Jewess from Kiev, volunteered to teach Russian to willing students among us, I jumped at the chance and spent most of my free time studying that language. My progress was so rapid that after a few weeks I could read and write Russian.

One day, our political commissar suggested that our group should produce a hostel magazine in Russian and hang it on the wall. To my surprise, I was nominated as editor. I accepted the position, got another fellow to help me, and in no time we produced a magazine. Of course, the dogmatic purity of each article was checked and double-checked by the commissar.

Our biggest problem was how to desist from criticising the actions of Nazi Germany. The commissar, who tried very hard to re-educate us, told us on many occasions that peace-loving Germany was being attacked by the imperialist countries of Poland, England, and France. We simply could not agree with him. He insisted that the Germans were allies of the Soviet Union, and that we would not be allowed to insult or unjustly portray the German leaders. He held to the official Soviet line that Poland was finished forever.

The friendly relations between Germany and the Soviet Union allowed us to send mail to the German-occupied territories of Poland. I wrote regularly to my parents and to Fela. However, I never got any replies from them. Incidentally, I also wrote a letter to my grandmother in Chicago. Within a very short time, I received a reply with a money draft enclosed. Although I needed the money badly, I could not accept the ridiculously low rate of exchange offered to me by the bank, and I asked them to send the money back to my grandmother Yitta in Chicago.

In March, I had an accident at work. My leg was injured when it was trapped between two trolleys, and I was on sick leave for three weeks. Then I was given a certificate stating that I should be employed in undertaking light duties, not underground. The only light duties they found for me on the surface were at a nearby stone quarry, where they prepared gravel for concrete. The labour was harder than in the mine, but the pay was only half of what I'd been earning previously, which even then had been barely enough to live on. In the quarry, I did not earn enough to pay for my food. To get extra money, I was forced to sell some of my meagre belongings at the market.

In April, the people in our group became restless. It was still very cold, and a lot of them were in the same situation as I was in — working hard, yet unable to survive on their poor earnings. One after another, they began to disappear, illegally. Most were heading towards the warmer regions of the Soviet Union. They bought train tickets to Moscow, where they hoped to obtain the necessary travel permits that would allow them to proceed to their chosen destinations. I was against breaking the contract, and I thought we should stay on. My cousin agreed with me wholeheartedly.

A few days later, my cousin, who was doing a lot better at work than most of the others, told me that he had changed his mind. He now believed that we had no future in Kizel and that we should leave as soon as possible. I could not envisage staying on without my cousin, and gave in. We began planning our departure. We needed money for the fare to Moscow and beyond, as well as for food on the road. My cousin had nothing worthwhile to sell, so I went to the market and sold my spare pair of trousers. We bought railway tickets, and were to leave on the evening of the next day.

The next morning, we did not go to work. In the afternoon, when we were all packed and ready, my cousin suddenly announced that he had reconsidered our position and thought that my original attitude was correct. Since the summer was not too far away, we could easily hold on until our contract expired in December. Then we would be legally able to pick any place in the Soviet Union to live and work in. Despite being mad at him for making me sell my trousers, I gave in. I did not want us to separate, and I was also happy that we would not be doing anything illegal.

The following three days, we went to work as if nothing had happened. On the evening of the third day, my cousin announced that he had had a change of heart again. A couple with whom he was friendly were leaving in a few hours' time. Since we could be ready at short notice, he thought that we should join them and travel together. This was too much for me to swallow. I became hysterical. I could not agree with him anymore. I told him to go by himself if he wanted to; I would stay.

Whatever else I told him did not stop him from leaving. He departed later that evening. During the next two days, I felt terribly depressed and lonely. I was devastated by my cousin's absence. I could not eat; I could not sleep. Then I learned that two more people in the hostel were preparing to depart. I made a hasty decision to join them. I still had my railway ticket to Moscow, and I hoped that I could find my cousin there, as he would be still waiting for his travel documents.

Chapter Six

THE TRIP TO Moscow was uneventful. At the large central railway station, we met a few people from our group. They had seen my cousin there, but, regretfully, I was too late. He was very lucky to have obtained a living permit for Tashkent, and had departed the previous evening. Knowing where he had gone still gave me some hope of catching up with him. For three days, I went from one bureaucrat to another, begging for a permit. The answer was the same everywhere: 'Go back to Kizel, honour your contract, then we will allow you to settle wherever you want.'

I felt miserable as I and my two travelling companions took a train to Kiev. We had been told that permits to stay and work in different parts of the Ukraine were being issued from there to some people. That seemed a lot better than the coalmine in Kizel. The railway station at Kiev was full of people in a similar situation to ours — returnees from different parts of that vast country. All my efforts to obtain a work permit in Kiev were fruitless. After three days, I joined a mass of people boarding a train travelling in the direction of the occupied Polish territories, now called Western

Byelorussia and Western Ukraine.

The next day, we stopped at the old Polish-Russian border town of Serniki. The local Jewish population was very sympathetic to our plight. While we waited for the next train, they offered us food and shelter. The same thing happened in Kowel. A few days later, early in May 1940, I arrived in Białystok, for the second time. This time I was alone, penniless, and disillusioned about my future prospects in the Soviet Union.

The situation in Białystok had changed. The synagogues and communal halls no longer accommodated refugees. Ogrodniczki was also closed to them. In February–March, the whole population, including refugees, had been ordered to apply for Soviet citizenship and passports. Once they received their passports, all refugees, except for some special party members, had to move to the interior of the Soviet Union. Refugees who did not want to take Soviet passports had to register for repatriation to the German-occupied territories of Poland.

As absurd as it seemed to me, large numbers of Jewish refugees preferred to go back home, in many cases to the already existing ghettos, rather than settle in the Soviet Union as Soviet citizens. They feared that they would be trapped there forever. Most of the people in Białystok who were waiting for repatriation had private accommodation and seemed to be making a good living. I needed some income, a job of any kind, and I also needed shelter. Yet I could not obtain them because I was an illegal returnee from the interior.

I found some casual work at the railway freight depot, where they did not ask for any documents. It was heavy labour — lugging 80-kilogram bags of wheat, flour, or sugar — but I did not mind doing it. The majority of people working there were returnees, like me. They were sheltering in a disused warehouse nearby, and they invited me to move in. I stayed there until the end of May, then joined a group of about twenty-five people, mostly returnees, who were going to work in a forest about fifty kilometres from Białystok.

A Jewish man from Minsk offered us work for the whole summer. The pay and accommodation were not too bad. There were a few couples among us, and the women were hired to do the cooking and housekeeping for the whole group. I was happy to get away from Białystok and find such a hideaway. We were living as if we were in a commune. The fresh air and good company made me forget the reality.

At the end of June, our employer, who was a good-hearted, kind man, despite being a party 'apparatchik', told us that the night before, the Internal Security people had rounded up all refugees staying in the territories of Western Byelorussia and Western Ukraine who did not have Soviet passports. They had been loaded into waiting trains and sent away to unknown destinations. He thought that they would be deported to outlying republics and put into restricted areas, under the authority of the Internal Security. The man assured us that for the time being we were safe in the forest, and that he would look after us.

In the middle of August, our employer warned us that he could not keep us much longer. The situation had changed for the worse, and he told us that we should be prepared to move out at short notice. A week later, we had to leave.

I spent a few days in a nearby village thinking about my future. Since I could not go on without a passport, I decided that I should present myself to the police voluntarily and apply for one. I would tell them that I had been working in the forest since arriving from Lodz in November, and that I had had no opportunity to get a passport there. I was sure that since all 'undesirable' refugees had been removed from the territories in the June round-up, the authorities would be quite willing to grant my request, as I was ready to move to the interior of the Soviet Union.

I arrived in Białystok late one afternoon and went to see the only person I knew there, my workmate from Lodz, Hersh Cukier. Being a prominent party member, he had been allowed to stay and work in Białystok. I told him about my plans, and asked him if he could put me up for one night only. Although he was not happy about it, because it was illegal, he nevertheless agreed to do so. He also wanted to see me the next day, if my plans were successful. Before I left him in the morning, I told him how worried my parents would be should they not receive any mail from me. He promised to write to them and to explain the situation, if I failed to come back from the police.

I went to the central police station and conveyed my request to the man in charge. He politely asked me to wait, but, two hours later, when I wanted to go out to buy some food, the policeman at the door would not allow me to leave. I understood then how naive I had been, how little I knew of the way the Soviet security forces behaved. Sometime later, I was interrogated at length by a senior officer, who patiently filled in a long form. Then he announced that I was under arrest for having illegally crossed the border of the Soviet Union in November 1939. He added that the punishment for my crime was not a heavy one — I would probably get a sentence of only three years' jail. A few years later, a dear friend of mine, a native of Homel, told me: 'In our country, if they want somebody, they'll always find a paragraph in the criminal law to suit him.'

When they brought me there, under guard, I soon found out why Ogrodniczki was closed. The familiar place had been turned into a prison camp for single people, mostly Jews, arrested during the June round-up. Two months later, they were still there, waiting for transport to the Gulags of the Soviet Union. After about two weeks, the orders for transportation arrived but, as I was a latecomer, my documents were not among them.

I was taken to the municipal prison of Białystok, where I stayed for a month. The living conditions there were extremely cramped. I was put in a cell that, according to regulations, should have held twelve people. They squeezed thirty men into it — people of different nationalities, common criminals, political detainees, and others. The criminals were the rulers. One had to follow their orders. Although the food was very bad, the lack of exercise and the poor standard of personal hygiene were our biggest problems.

At the beginning of October, I was taken to the railway

station in a group of about twenty-five people, and loaded into a train guarded by soldiers. We disembarked in a town called Orsha, in Byelorussia, and were marched to the local prison. The three weeks I stayed there were very educational. The place was less crowded. We could wash and exercise every day, and we had a shower once a week. The food, although it consisted of regulation prison rations, was much better than in Białystok. In my cell, I met a number of very interesting people of many nationalities, from all walks of life. One of them was a Seventh Day Adventist: a man in his fifties, fluent in five languages, and the holder of an MA in philosophy. He told me that since the October Revolution, the best sons and daughters of Russia could be found in the prisons and Gulags, not outside. In a short time, I learned a lot about life in the Soviet Union.

At the end of October, the documents for my group at last arrived. We left Orsha in a heavily guarded train and travelled north, in the direction of Leningrad and the Gulf of Finland. The next day we arrived at 'Gulag 425', one of the compounds surrounded by barbed wire and guard towers, in a vast complex of corrective-labour camps that stretched for miles along the sea shore. They housed 120,000 prisoners. Apparently, the top military brass of the Soviet Union had decided to fortify the whole length of the Gulf of Finland. The cheapest way to build the fortifications was with slave labour. Thus, an appropriate order was given to the Internal Security. They quickly established the camps and filled them with the necessary human resources — prisoners, of course.

Chapter Seven

OUR CAMP held 450 men. To my great surprise, we were all Jewish, with just one exception. Most of the prisoners were like myself: refugees who had been Polish citizens. They had been arrested during the June round-ups in the new Soviet territories, and had been brought to this newly established camp in July.

Everyone, except for a few service tradesmen, like a barber, a tailor, and a cobbler, as well as the doctor, went out to work on the fortifications. The daily routine never varied. Reveille was at 6.00 a.m.: we got dressed; received the daily bread ration; ate breakfast, which consisted of two spoonfuls of cooked cereal and as much boiled water as one wanted; and assembled in brigades near the gate of the compound. Each brigade was counted and recounted as we were led out for the eight-kilometre march, surrounded by armed guards with dogs. The usual warning was: 'Keep in close formation during the march — anyone moving away three steps, in any direction, will be shot without a further warning.' The brigades and the men in charge of them, the brigade leaders, were central to the daily life of the camp inmates. Since the amount of the most essential of the food rations, bread, varied according to the output of work performed, having a clever and friendly brigade leader, who knew which jobs to take on and how to organise his labour and fill in the work reports, meant the difference between starving and surviving.

I was lucky with my first brigade. The brigade leader's name was Reisen; he was a man in his early thirties, a native of Vilno. I asked him if he was a relation of Avrom Reisen, the great Yiddish poet. He told me quietly that Avrom was his uncle, a brother of his father, Zalmen Reisen, a well-known Yiddish writer and educator, and one of the founders of YIVO. Since he, too, was a graduate of the CJSZO schools, my brigade leader took an immediate liking to me. For the two months he had me under his wing, I was a sort of protégé. He made sure that, whenever possible, I got a little extra food.

In November, the weather turned nasty. It rained every day, and the howling, cold Arche winds penetrated right through our bodies. We came home from work in sodden clothes, yet lacked the facilities to have them dried during the night. In the morning, we were marched out to work in the same wet clothing. More and more people became sick as the frosts set in, yet the camp doctor was forbidden to allow sick leave to more than ten inmates per day. We continued the daily routine of working in the open, on the fortifications.

One morning in January, I felt so sick that I could not get up at all. The camp doctor had one look at me, took my temperature, and told the clerk to take me to the central hospital immediately. I was semi-delirious, and woke up the following morning in a white-lined bed, covered with two clean blankets. At lunch, I was offered white bread. It was a paradise on earth. After a few days, I felt a lot better. Regretfully, they could not keep me longer than ten days. I was discharged and given a certificate stating that for the next two months I should be given light duties only.

The only light duty the new brigade leader found for me was pushing trolleys of gravel all day at the building site of the fortifications. The bread ration on the new job was half of the previous one. I was always hungry, and became weaker from day to day.

Our camp kitchen was run by outsiders — Russian prisoners from other camps. Every evening, after dinner, which consisted of a bowl of soup, a queue of volunteer kitchen-helpers for the all-night shift formed near the entrance. It was known that in the morning each helper received a full billy of cooked cereal topped with eating oil. For weeks, I resisted the temptation. The main reason was that after working all night in the kitchen, one had to march out with the brigade and work all day again.

Hunger, however, is immune to reason. I kept on thinking about one thing only — how to fill my stomach, how not to feel hungry, just once. One evening, I volunteered for the night's work. First, we scrubbed the kettles and cleaned the stoves; then we peeled potatoes all night, under the watchful eye of a cook, who didn't trust us too much. At last the reveille sounded and all the helpers lined up for their reward. I was given a full one-gallon billy of kasha cereal topped with cooking oil. I then went to my brigade leader and picked up my bread ration, which I decided to save for later. I sat down and began eating my cereal, watched and envied by many hungry people. I ate and ate, and kept on eating until I had finished the lot.

As we assembled at the gate, I already felt a little bloated. The eight-kilometre march seemed to take a lot longer than usual. I felt awful. I was so heavy that I could not lift my legs. When we arrived at the work place, I was not fit for anything, except running to the toilet, then lying down. Never again did I volunteer for kitchen work.

The temperature dropped to around 30 degrees below zero. Our clothing offered us little protection against the cold. The harsh frost and the constantly biting wind played havoc with the health of all the inmates, even the strongest among us. By the beginning of February, it was evident that few of us would survive the winter if we were to be forced to keep on working in the open, on the fortifications.

Our salvation came from an unexpected quarter. One morning, all the brigades were stopped at the gate and told to return to the barracks. When we were all assembled in the huge hall, a major from Internal Security, who looked Jewish, entered with four junior officers. He began his speech by abusing us and accusing us of counter-revolutionary activities and industrial sabotage. Then he threatened each of us with extra sentences and other punishments. In the end, he told us that a decision had been made about the remaining winter months. The tradesmen among us — tailors, bootmakers, carpenters, and furniture makers — would be directed to enlarge their workshops and to gainfully employ all the inmates of the compound. He added that the output from our workshops would be distributed among the whole camp complex and that we would not go back to the fortifications until May.

We were saved. I became an apprentice bootmaker. The materials we used were worn tyres for soles and canvas for uppers. The finished product wasn't very comfortable or long-lasting, but it was good enough for prisoners. We worked inside, but we were hungrier than ever. The simple arithmetic used by Internal Security was that, being inside, our bodies needed fewer calories. Accordingly, they cut our previous, already meagre, rations. We were all warm and dry, but starving.

Spring arrived at last, towards the end of April. Strangely enough, everybody wanted to work outside again, not to be cooped up in the barracks. At the beginning of May, new brigades were formed, and we went out to work on the fortifications again. As the weather improved and summer arrived, the work seemed easier, and our spirits rose. We were still hungry, but we somehow got used to camp life and made the best of it.

22 June 1941. Reveille sounded as usual. After breakfast, the brigades assembled at the gate, waiting for the guards. It took them a lot longer to arrive than on any other day. Then the chief of the guards told us to go back to the barracks, that there would be no work that day. No one could understand why we had got a day off; it had never happened before. In the afternoon, we were told to assemble outside. Our camp

commander announced that, early that morning, the Soviet Union had been treacherously attacked by the armed forces of Germany; that battles were raging along all the borders; that we might come under bombardment from the German air force; and that we were to stay in the barracks, awaiting further orders.

It was a real surprise for us, too. The two allies had fallen out at last. The following day, we saw a dogfight between two aeroplanes in the sky, far away. On the third day, an order came that all camps in the Gulf of Finland, including ours, were to be evacuated immediately. A train arrived, and we were loaded into it. All the windows were covered with barbed wire, and each wagon was heavily guarded by Internal Security soldiers. We travelled eastward for about four weeks on the grossly disorganised railway system. The heat inside the carriage was oppressive, and the supply of food, as well as water, was sporadic. One morning, we were told to disembark. The name of the place was Karaganda, in northern Kazakhstan.

The Karaganda camp was a huge transit centre for prisoners from the whole region. For the first time, we found ourselves among the general camp population, from which we had been insulated until then. As in all Soviet camps, the criminals, especially the young ones among them, were the internal rulers. Unless one did what they said, one could lose everything, be beaten up, or, if it came to it, even killed.

Usually, people did not stay long in the transit camp. In our case, however, an unexpected event occurred. Shortly after our arrival, an amnesty for all previous Polish citizens was announced. The Polish government-in-exile and the Soviet government had signed an agreement to that effect. All Polish citizens in prisons, camps, and forced internment were to be released as soon as possible. The fit males of military age were requested to enlist in the Polish army that was being formed in the Soviet Union to fight Nazi Germany, alongside the Soviet armies.

We were very excited by this new turn of events. However, since we could not be allocated to work brigades because of our forthcoming release, our daily rations, as for all non-performing prisoners, were drastically reduced. We waited impatiently for the longed-for day of freedom, but, in the meantime, we were starving.

At last, in the first week of September, the release documents arrived. One by one, our people were called to the guard house to receive a release certificate, travel vouchers, a few roubles, and rations for the trip. The majority chose as their destination the warmer Asian republics of the USSR.

Again, as had caused problems for me earlier in Białystok, I was in a group of twenty-five people who lacked Soviet residence papers. All our complaints were dismissed. We had to wait for another six long weeks. We were hungry and weak, and could hardly walk by the time our documents arrived, in the second half of October. The Asian republics were out of bounds by then, as well as anywhere west of the Ural Mountains. We were told that we could choose any other place, as long as it was in Siberia.

A mate of mine, a young engineering graduate from

Warsaw whose father had survived World War I in a POW camp in a place called Biysk, in the Altai region of southern Siberia, suggested that we should go there. So we chose Biysk. We got our release papers, all our entitlements, and off we went, as free citizens. Fifteen months of imprisonment had come to an end.

Chapter Eight

THE BIYSK RAILWAY STATION was packed with freed Polish citizens when we arrived there at the end of October. Among them was a group of Polish citizens, non-Jews, led by a woman called Mrs Marczak. Her husband, a major in the Polish army, had escaped from the Germans after the September war in 1939, and made it to London. The woman asked me where I had come from and where I was heading. At first, she suggested that I should enlist in the Polish army, but then she corrected herself, saying that, the way I looked, I would not pass the medical. (Actually, she did not know that the Polish army had already stopped accepting Jewish applicants, except for a few officers. The old anti-Semitic prejudices of the Poles were still alive.)

Mrs Marczak had probably taken a liking to me, and she suggested that I would be welcome to join her group. They were going to a sugar mill, about fifteen kilometres away. The men were fully experienced in that sort of work, having done it for years in Poland. She negotiated a contract with the mill to house them and to provide work for all of them. I accepted her offer, and the following day I went with the group.

The first two months at the sugar mill were very hard for me. On arrival, I was accommodated in a hostel for single men, all strangers. I was weak and I had no money. On top of that, I was given outside work, pushing mountains of stocked sugar beet into the water channels that floated them into the mill for processing. The cold weather soon set in, but I was supplied with protective clothing. Little by little, I got my strength back, in a large measure thanks to the sugar beet, which tasted delicious when baked, and was a good supplement to my everyday diet. After a few weeks, I was transferred to work inside the mill.

Things were looking up. I could get into the refining department and taste the finished product. Like all Soviet citizens, I also found a way to take some sugar home. Just a little in the beginning, but later, more and more — enough to sell, and, with the money obtained, to buy other things I needed. The only way to survive in that system was to do something illegal. Everyone, from the top brass to the lowest-paid street cleaner did it, each in a different way.

Most of the Poles that I came with were friendly towards me. One family in particular often asked me to visit them, and treated me like one of their own. They were a middle-aged couple with three grown-up children, the oldest boy about my age. They knew that I was suffering because of the lack of news from my family in Poland, and showed a genuine interest in me, trying hard to alleviate my loneliness. On every holiday they invited me, at least once, for a special family meal. I could not vouch how they felt about Jews in general, but I believed that their friendship was genuine. We remained good friends until I left Biysk.

I settled in quite well in Biysk. A few months after my arrival, three Jewish men, also Polish refugees, but a little older than me, came to work at our mill. It felt good to have mates again. Some time later, I found private accommodation and moved out of the hostel. I only had a bed in the corner of a room, but I had a lot more privacy than in the hostel. The landlady, whose husband was at the front, had a boy of about five. The rent I paid supplemented her income, and she very much appreciated it when I gave her some sugar, which I brought home often. As the first anniversary of my coming to Biysk approached, I had to admit that the past year had been a good one.

The mill management needed men for the boilermaking department, which had the task of maintaining and overhauling the plant and equipment of the whole enterprise. I was twenty and looked very fit. One day, the chief engineer told me that he had transferred me there. I did not like it. It would mean harder work and no sugar in the future, but there was nothing I could do about it. I became a boilermaker's assistant.

The equipment used was very crude. The cutting and bending of the sheet metal, and then the fastening of it, was done manually, in most cases. It was strenuous physical labour. There were seven of us altogether — two elderly tradesmen and five assistants. The other four assistants were ethnic Poles from the Ukrainian region formerly in eastern Poland: burly peasant types who had been imprisoned by the Soviet police for criminal offences. They, too, had benefited from the amnesty, like all other Polish citizens. At the beginning, they teased me a little. However, I made a great effort to keep up with them, and they soon accepted me as an equal. That meant I had to drink with them — not just a little, but a lot. Vodka was not cheap on the black market. When I asked them where they got all their money, they told me they would tell me soon how I, too, could make some extra money.

I saw him for the first time in the canteen, in the autumn of 1942. Three of us were sitting at a table, eating, and talking in Yiddish. A short, old-looking man, with a red beard, a covered head, and one arm in a splint, asked us in a tearful, low voice if he could join us. He explained that he had not heard a Yiddish word for many years.

His name was Lyova and he had just arrived from a Gulag, where he had been incarcerated since 1935. His original sentence had been for ten years, but he was released after serving just over seven years. He had come to our settlement the day before, and he had been given a job as night watchman in the mill's chicken farm. Lyova invited me to visit him any evening, and we became very good friends.

A native of Homel, in Soviet Byelorussia, Lyova was only thirty-seven years old, but he had made himself look much older and feigned the injured hand, to be safe from an army call-up. He told me that he had left behind a wife, who was a doctor, and a daughter of two, when he was arrested on a trumped-up charge of being a Zionist and a counter-revolutionary. Lyova was brought up in a traditional Jewish, well-to-do merchant family, and he had received a good religious and secular education. After the revolution, their life had changed completely. Being so-called 'capitalists', his family was harassed and persecuted. Under the new regime, no one could be trusted anymore. In fact, the man who investigated him after his arrest was a childhood and school friend.

Lyova's life-story was tragic. As the German army advanced towards Homel in the summer of 1941, Lyova's wife lost a leg in the heavy bombardment that took place during the hurried evacuation. Their daughter, an only child, was fatally injured, and died in the arms of her mother. Through all his years of imprisonment, Lyova had kept in touch with his wife through an intermediary, just in case letters from a counter-revolutionary might endanger her. At the moment, she lived and worked in Alma-Ata, the capital of Kazakhstan. After his release from the camp, his freedom was restricted to the Altai region. The authorities would not give him a travel permit to Alma-Ata. Through Lyova, I got a deeper insight into the Soviet way of life. He made me think a lot.

Halfway between our sugar mill and Biysk, there was a meat-processing plant. From time to time, I walked to the town to buy something at the market or to meet Jewish people who had stalls there. Passing near the meat works, I got acquainted with a Jewish family — a mother and two daughters — who worked there and lived nearby. One of the daughters was married to a man who was away, mobilised into a labour battalion. The second daughter, the younger one, was about my age. There was another girl of a similar age living with them. She was a good friend from their hometown near Warsaw, and she had joined them when they fled Poland.

They invited me to drop in whenever I could, and I accepted the invitation with pleasure. I found in their home a family atmosphere, which I missed so much. I usually brought them some sugar, and we would have a cup of tea and talk for a while. Sometimes, I was asked to join them for a meal, too. I thoroughly enjoyed those visits and believed that they did, likewise. I never thought of getting into a permanent relationship with a Jewish girl. My heart was with Fela, my sweetheart, my first and only love, whom I had promised to come back to after the war. Of course, I was a healthy young man and I had a normal, male sexual drive. However, the only relationships with women I allowed myself were casual, or of a non-binding nature.

One day, when I came to visit the family, I immediately felt that there was something wrong. I did not stay long and left, under some pretext. The girl staying in the household, the friend of the family, caught up with me on the street. She was obviously distressed. Sobbing, she told me that a serious row had taken place, just before I came, and it was about me. The mother and daughters had accused her of flirting with me, and of being the reason why I had not yet proposed to the younger daughter. The girl was very surprised when I burst into laughter after she finished her story.

After that event, I still continued my friendship with the family, but my visits were rare and brief.

My workmates at the boilermaker's shop asked me one day if I wanted to make some real money. I said I did. They explained that on a few previous occasions they had managed to gain access to the sugar store in the mill, from where they had stolen a few sacks of sugar each time. If I could provide them with a safe hiding place for the sacks and then find a reliable buyer for the stuff, I could get a hefty cut from the operation. They thought that I should have no trouble finding a willing buyer among the Jews of Biysk.

I asked my mentor, Lyova, what he thought about it. He had a ready answer. If my workmates could deliver the stuff to him at the chicken farm, for a pre-arranged price, he would hide it there, in the cellar, for a while. Then we would get a buyer from town. However, the Ukrainians would have to trust us. We could not pay them until the sugar was sold.

I explained our proposition to the Ukrainians, and they agreed immediately. They trusted me completely. A few weeks later, they did the 'job', and I helped them bring six 80-kilogram sacks of sugar to Lyova's place. Everything went well. I got my cut, Lyova got his, and they got their full payment, as agreed. Even the sugar store manager was happy. We were told by an inside source that he had reported ten sacks missing. That allowed him to sell four sacks on the black market and to split the proceeds with his cronies higher-up. We repeated the operation three more times.

As the year 1943 progressed, the situation on the eastern front changed drastically. After their humiliating defeat at Stalingrad, the German armies had lost the initiative and were now retreating along the whole length of the front. The Soviet forces began to liberate the towns and villages of the occupied territories. All the newspapers carried stories of great suffering in the civilian population during the German occupation. However, there was very little information about the fate of the Jews. It seemed that there were simply no Jews left. Only sporadic eyewitness accounts of atrocities committed against them by the Germans appeared in the press.

In April, the radio mentioned an uprising in the Warsaw ghetto. The May issue of the Polish monthly, issued by the recently formed Union of Polish Patriots, contained a lot of detail about the heroic but hopeless struggle of the Jewish fighters in the burning ghetto. We knew very little about what was happening in the other ghettos of Poland, but my worst fears about the fate of my family seemed to have been realised. Until then, I had still hoped that they and Fela would somehow survive. There was not much hope left after the Warsaw Ghetto Uprising.

The leader of the Polish army in the Soviet Union, General Anders, and the Soviet military command could not agree on the role of the Polish army in the war with Germany. After lengthy, unsuccessful negotiations, General Anders was allowed to evacuate his whole army, which he was to incorporate into the British armed forces. They soon crossed the border into Iran. The families of the officers went with them.

The Union of Polish Patriots, a Soviet-inspired organisation established under the leadership of Wanda Wasilewska in Moscow, quickly announced the formation of a new Polish army, to fight alongside the Soviet army. The nucleus of the First Polish Army, under the command of Colonel (later General) Zygmunt Berling, came into being in mid-1943, and all previous Polish citizens of military age were to be called up to serve in it.

In January 1944, I received a notice requiring me to volunteer to enlist. The sons of my Polish friends were also called up. On the eve of our departure, the Poles organised a send-off party, to which I was invited. Naturally, there was plenty of vodka, and I drank a little more than I should have. The next morning, when somebody woke me up, I was not feeling too well. We had a fifteen-kilometre walk to the army office, in town. It was very cold outside, and the ground was covered with a thick layer of snow About midway, we passed through a small forest. I felt so tired that I could not walk any further. I told the group that I needed a little rest, and they went on. I sat down on a tree stump, fell asleep, and woke up in the evening. It was too late to proceed to the city, so I walked back home, and early the following morning I hurried to the army office.

I apologised for being late, and truthfully explained the reason. They told me that my group had already left, and asked me to wait inside. I waited for two days. On the third day, they sent me home, saying they would call me for the next intake. Although my Polish friends understood and believed my explanation, I did not feel too comfortable in their company at that time. When news came in the spring that the new recruits to the Polish forces had suffered heavy casualties in their first battle, I felt even worse. One of our boys was killed, and two of them came back, a little later, injured.

I missed taking part in that battle by pure accident. Not long afterwards, my job in the mill was reclassified as being of an essential nature, and I was given an exemption from future Polish army enlistment campaigns.

The days dragged on, turned into weeks, then stretched into months of grey reality in wartime Siberia. Life was a matter of bare existence only, of following a daily routine, like an automaton. There was not much else one could do. The global conflict and the Soviet system made us, the refugees, feel very vulnerable and unable to look forward. The future seemed to be very bleak for us.

6 June 1944 began as any other day. The wake-up siren sounded, as usual, at 7.00 a.m. I rose and looked outside, through the window. It was a perfect early-summer morning, mild and still, the sun already up. I washed and dressed, had some breakfast, and left my lodgings about 7.45 a.m. My 12-hour shift started at 8.00 a.m. The distance to the sugar mill was about a mile. I walked briskly, meeting a number of workmates on the way. Pretty soon, I was engaged in customary small talk with a few of them. As we approached the large administrative building, we could hear the radio

loudspeakers at full blast, but could not yet understand the words. These broadcasts of the official news bulletins were our main source of information.

Lately, the war news had been much better. The Germans were still retreating, after suffering heavy defeats. Nearly all of Byelorussia and Ukraine had been liberated, and the Soviet armies were continuing their thrust westward. The Western allies were doing well, too. They had marched into Rome, and were poised to liberate the whole of Italy. My mounting optimism about the outcome of the war, about the total destruction of Nazi Germany, seemed to be fully justified now.

As the words of the news bulletin became clear, my heartbeat accelerated. The speaker announced that, early that morning, the Western allies' armies had successfully crossed the Channel and landed in Normandy. The long-awaited second European front had at last become a reality. The liberation of Europe from Nazi occupation had now entered into the final stage. I could not hold back the tears in my eyes. Four-and-a-half years had passed since I had left home at seventeen. During all those years spent in the Soviet Union, I had not been able to communicate with my dear ones, and knew nothing about their fate. The hope of a swift, decisive defeat of the Nazis, and the possibility of returning, had now taken concrete shape.

I was eager to start the day's work, and walked briskly into the large hall, towards the engineering department. The foreman explained the job on hand to our team. We had to lower a large metal tank from a platform, about six metres above the ground, thoroughly clean it inside and out, replace all the worn parts, and then lift it back to its previous position. After a short discussion, we began our task. Four hoists were secured onto the ceiling metal rafters, and four of us climbed up to the platform. Each man had to handle one hoist. Another team member would give instructions from above the platform, and the foreman would co-ordinate the whole job from the floor. Before the tank could be lowered, it had to be lifted and pushed outward. That part of the job needed particular care. Each of the four hoists had to bear an equal strain.

The operation went as planned, until the tank was raised to the desired height. Then, for some unknown reason, the chain holding my hoist suddenly snapped. My hoist plunged down and I followed, in a split second, head first towards the concrete floor.

When I opened my eyes, I was lying on the floor with blood streaming from my scalp and my left arm hurting badly. Around me, in a circle, stood dozens of people. In their eyes I could see an expression of pity as well as resignation. I closed my eyes again. I thought: *Yes, they are right. This is the end of the road for me. I will not survive, but why did it have to happen today, on a morning full of joy and hope? The war will end soon, but I shall never again see my family or sweetheart. At twenty-two, I am finished.* Then I lost consciousness.

Some time afterwards, I woke up in the first-aid room. A nurse was bandaging my head, then she put my broken wrist in a splint and the whole arm in a special support. She smiled and apologised, saying that she could not do anything more for me and that I would have to go to the hospital in the city for further treatment. There they would stitch up my scalp and set the wrist in plaster. She assured me that I should be all right otherwise, and added that I was very lucky — I would be off work for at least a month that summer.

The nurse went to the desk drawer and handed me a form, stamped and signed by the managing director of the mill. The certificate stated that I was temporarily disabled, and entitled me to retain all rations and pay until declared fit to work. I was lucky indeed. For the next six weeks, the weather was magnificent. Being right-handed, I was able to indulge in fishing every day, in the nearby river Biya. Although I was not very experienced in the sport, and had very rudimentary equipment, I caught some large pike every day.

The nurse was right. My injuries were mending, although slowly. The weather was good, and I enjoyed the enforced holiday. However, during the third week, a very disturbing event occurred. One of my Ukrainian co-workers was arrested, caught stealing boxes of cheese from a riverboat. He did not need the cheese or the money that he would make from selling it. Stealing was in his blood; he had done it all his life, and he was bored with a long lay-off from stealing sugar.

As soon as I told Lyova about this, he thought that we might be in trouble. He knew the system well. For a long time, the police had suspected the Ukrainians of being behind the missing sugar. They had arrested them a few times, but had to release them because of a lack of evidence. This time, they had one of them, caught red-handed. Lyova was sure that the police would not stop before they made the Ukrainian admit all his previous sins. He was convinced that, if this happened, both of us needed to be prepared to make a hasty departure from Biysk.

I knew a woman who was a cleaner at the local police station, where Vaska, our Ukrainian friend, was held. I went to see the cleaner, and she agreed to give me and the other Ukrainians daily reports of the situation. If possible, she would also bring messages to and from Vaska. The interrogation dragged on for weeks. At the beginning he held out well, but the woman thought that he would not last for very long. I went to see Lyova every day, and we worked out a contingency departure plan.

In the middle of July came the news of an advance by the Soviet army into Poland. The Polish army was taking part in the liberation of the territory, and was nearing the Vistula river. The city of Lublin became the seat of the provisional government of the new Polish Republic. I went to the managing director of the mill and asked him, since I would remain unfit to work for some time yet, to give me an official release from the mill and a permit to travel to Lublin, to join the Polish army, after my injuries healed. Of course, my main goal was to leave Biysk legally, and soon, but I did want to fight the Germans in the Polish army.

The chief executive, a Ukrainian Jew, was a zealous party member. He gave me a sermon about the superiority of the

Soviet system and the achievements of the revolution, and he advised me to forget about returning to Poland, ever. As far as he was concerned, Poland was going to be like the Soviet Union, and I might as well stay in Biysk. He flatly refused my request.

A week later, I learned that Vaska's resistance had been broken. He was a shadow of his former self and had begun to talk. That same evening, Lyova and I fled Biysk, carrying very little luggage. To avoid train travel, where permits were required, we walked along the river for about twenty kilometres, to the next boarding point for the river boats. We arrived there in good time to catch a boat going to Barnaul, the capital of the Altai region. No questions were asked while we were boarding, and no questions were asked when we disembarked in Barnaul, three days later. Everything went as planned.

Chapter Nine

ANOTHER CHAPTER of my life began. I needed new documents that would allow me to stay in Barnaul. In the Soviet Union during wartime, it was obligatory for each adult to have an ID card and a booklet showing his military status. Before we left Biysk, a fellow I knew gave me an address of a friend in Barnaul. I went there with Lyova, and we were told that, yes, they could help us. His daughter knew somebody in the police ID card office who would issue the documents to us, for 10,000 roubles each. He asked us to come back next day with photographs, whatever personal data we wanted to use, and half of the money. The balance was to be paid on delivery of the documents.

Everything went well, and a few days later we got our documents. After some consideration, I decided not to change my name or other personal data, except that I put in Kizel not Biysk as my previous place of residence. I figured that the police communications were not that efficient to warrant changing my name. There was one problem, though, with the military booklet. In Biysk, I had an exemption from being required to enlist in the Polish army; in Barnaul, I could be targetted for enlistment at any time. Lyova thought that it would be safer for us to split up. He made up his mind to join his wife in Alma-Ata. We wished each other good luck for the future, and off he went. I was alone again. Having spent the major part of my savings on the documents, I had to earn a living. Yet I was not comfortable staying in the city, only a few hundred kilometres from Biysk. Unexpectedly, a solution to the problem came along. In the Polish Community Centre, I met up again with my first friend in Biysk, Mrs Marczak, who was in charge of welfare. Within a few minutes she told me not to worry; she would help me. The centre had to prepare firewood for the winter for all the Polish welfare institutions. They had been given an allotment in a forest, fifty kilometres away. A group of twenty-five people was being organised for the job, which would last six weeks, at least. We would be well fed, accommodated in cabins, and paid at the end, with two overseas parcels of products and clothing. I thanked her, and signed up on the spot.

This was just what I needed. As far as I was concerned, it was a godsend. I was away from the city, had a well-paid job, and my companions were terrific. As it turned out, quite a few of the other workers were in a similar situation to me, wanting to lay low for a while. We lived as if in a commune: we worked together, ate together, and entertained ourselves in the evenings. It lasted until the end of September. After we received and sold the contents of our parcels, eight young men, including me, decided to join the Polish army in Lublin. Without travel permits, we could obtain train tickets for short distances only, but we hoped to get to Lublin, one way or another.

As it happened, we only made it to Novosibirsk, about 250 kilometres away. As soon as we stepped outside the railway station to buy some food, we were surrounded by Internal Security soldiers who were making a routine check of male travellers — looking for army deserters and anybody else whose documents were not 100 per cent in order. We were taken to the army office and told that, as we wanted to enlist in the Polish army, we should also be happy to serve in the Soviet army, since both of them were fighting the same enemy. Our complaint, that legally we could only be required to serve in the Polish army, was brushed aside. The next day, we were driven to a huge military compound, thirty kilometres away, and inducted into the Red Army.

We were handed old, worn uniforms, and for the first three weeks in October we underwent intensive military training, practically around the clock. Then we were dispatched to a collective farm in northern Kazakhstan, to help clear the grain harvest from the fields. We came back on 7 November to take part in the traditional military parade in honour of the anniversary of the October Revolution.

It was terribly cold, and we shivered as we waited for the general to arrive. At last he came and began the inspection of the assembled units. As the general was passing our unit and asking the usual question, 'Any complaints, boys?', I was pushed from behind by my Jewish mates, and found myself face to face with him. I told him that there were eight Polish citizens in our unit, who demanded to be sent to the Polish army, as was our legal right. His reply was: 'It's not important, soldier. Step back into line.'

The intensive military training continued. I was given an automatic rifle, and I had to work very hard to master it — not just the mechanics of loading and firing, but also how to maintain it and how to repair it when it got jammed, which happened very often. Towards the end of December, we were issued with new uniforms and told that we should be prepared for immediate departure to the front line. Indeed, a train was ready the next day. Each soldier was called by name and assigned to a specific carriage. For one reason or another, our group of eight was split up among the whole train. Only one of my mates was with me: Moyshe, a fellow from eastern Galicia, who was at least fifteen years older than me.

We were resigned to our fate. The time of the train's departure approached. Suddenly, our names were called out loudly by a sergeant outside. He told us to take our gear and come with him to the office. To our great surprise, our whole group of eight was taken off the train. Although the general had not admitted it at the time, our complaint was justified. He knew it, and gave the order not to send us to the front. All of us were excited as we entered the office, expecting to be sent to the Polish army immediately. Instead, we had to change back into the worn old uniforms, go to the barracks, and wait for further instructions.

We did not have to wait long. The military authorities decided that even if they could not keep us in active service in the Red Army, this did not mean they should release us. They devised a plan to include us in the next transport of medically unfit soldiers, which was being assembled in the compound, as military labour battalions. Thus they could send us wherever they wanted to, for what was practically slave labour, under army control. That seemed to be a very bleak future. There were among us a few who had actually fled such battalions in previous years. Our mood changed to despair.

There was nothing we could do to alter the situation. We were still soldiers under army rules, and had to follow orders. On 30 December, we were loaded onto a train carrying a detachment of 450 people. After passing Novosibirsk, the train continued in a south-easterly direction, arriving at the railway station of Stalinsk (now called Novokuznetsk) late in the evening of the following day. We were told to wait at the station for another train that would take us to our destination — a forest 250 kilometres away.

As Moyshe and I moved around the station, we met a few local Jews, refugees from Poland. When they heard where we were heading, they strongly advised us not to go. According to them, there was no way out from that place; it was literally the end of the road. They understood our situation and the risks involved, but insisted that we should not be on the train when it left Stalinsk.

And we weren't. We hid wherever possible around the station on that cold night of 1 January 1945. In the morning, we took a tram to the city. As advised by the locals, we went to the market and asked for a particular Jewish fellow. The man was very friendly, and immediately understood our plight. We were in military uniforms and without any documents. In order to survive — to draw rations and to find accommodation — we had to legalise our existence. The good man sent us to another, who gave us an address and the name of a manager who was working in the largest industrial and building enterprise in Stalinsk.

We arrived there too early. It was bitterly cold outside as we waited for the office to open. A woman came out and asked us who we were waiting for. She recognised that we were Jewish, invited us in, and offered us a cup of tea. A Jewess from Bessarabia, she worked as a concierge at the building, and she knew the man we were waiting for very well. Her assurances that he would help us raised our hopes and lifted our spirits.

The man we were waiting for, comrade Alexander Yefimovich Rozinsky, was a native of Kiev; a good party member, but also a man with a warm Jewish heart. After we told him our true story in Russian, he asked us one question in Yiddish: were we on the run from active army service? He could help us if we had fled the labour battalion, but would not if we had deserted the army. We assured him that we were telling him the truth. He smiled and said not to worry, that everything would be fine, and rang somebody in the building to come to see him.

A man in military uniform came in. Comrade Rozinsky presented us as two people missing from his previous group of compulsorily called-up workers, and asked the man to legalise our military and civil status. Then he wrote an order to the personnel department, asking them to issue us with ration coupons, protective clothing, and accommodation in a hostel for single men. Before we left, he wished us good luck and told us to present ourselves for work in their railway department, in two days' time.

We were civilians again, had a roof over our heads, and had a job, too. Not a very elegant or well-paid job, but it was not too bad for a start. We were loading coal onto company locomotives. The vast enterprise was in the middle of building a power station, aluminium works, and a huge non-ferrous metals foundry. It had its own locomotives to distribute the supplies of materials on its extensive rail network, stretching for many kilometres. Moyshe and I were assigned to the railway depot, which also served as an office for the traffic-movement controller. Our job was to refill the locomotives with coal when they arrived. We had to do it fairly quickly, too. It was dirty, strenuous physical labour, but I did not mind it at all. It was Moyshe who kept complaining.

As soon as we finished loading a locomotive, we could relax until another came along. Moyshe just stretched out on a seat and had a nap. I would usually go inside and watch the controller and his clerk at work. I was curious and interested. In no time, I could deputise for both of them. The controller used to disappear for quite a while, and smell of vodka when he returned. On many occasions, I had to answer the phone. Sometimes, it was the head of the department on the line, asking for details of freight, the position of locomotives, or the times of turn-around of the government railway rolling stock. There were occasions when I spent most of my time, especially on night shift, doing the work of the controller.

The head of the department was comrade Kurochkin, a

Ukrainian from Kharkov. He was a long-serving party member, with a distinguished career in several positions. When the Germans approached Kharkov, he had fled, on orders of the party, leaving his family behind. They had survived the German occupation, and, since his birthplace was liberated, he had applied to the party leadership many times for permission to return, to join his family. On every occasion, the pretext for refusal was that he must first find a person to replace him as head of the department. Kurochkin was quite a clever man. He knew that only a party member would be given his job. However, he thought that this rule would not apply to a temporary department head. Of course, I only got to know about all these things later.

About four weeks after we began to work in the railway department, comrade Kurochkin called me to his office. He told me that he had been following my progress with great interest, that I was a capable, literate, and intelligent person, and that he was prepared to appoint me as his deputy, if I agreed. That was a silly question. I agreed immediately; it was a much better job than loading coal into locomotives, and much cleaner, too. He showed me my desk in his office, and took me around to meet the other members of his staff. I was to start the new job the next day.

One person unhappy about my promotion was Moyshe. He could not understand how I could accept the new job while he was to remain in the depot, loading coal. We had been mates since we had met in the army, early in October the previous year. According to his way of thinking, I should have insisted on him, too, being given a job in the office.

This was despite the fact that he was practically illiterate in Russian and couldn't even speak it properly. Perhaps he clung to me because I was so fluent in Russian and was able to express myself eloquently in Yiddish and in Polish. Moyshe had lived all his life in a small town, and had made a living dealing in grain with the peasants. He had a good business brain, and always found a way to make money.

Comrade Kurochkin taught me everything he could in the shortest possible time. After four weeks, he applied to the party for a transfer to Kharkov, stating that he had a deputy who could fill in his position until a permanent head of the department was found. His request was granted, and for the next four weeks, until the arrival of comrade Verdomitsky, I was the acting head of the railway department.

Chapter Ten

LODZ WAS LIBERATED by the Soviet forces in the middle of January 1945. There was not much news on the radio or in the press about life in the freed city. The Polish monthly did publish some sporadic reports from different cities in Poland. There were stories of the death camps of Maidanek, Sobibor, Auschwitz, and others, but they did not convey the magnitude of the disaster that had befallen the Jews trapped in the German-occupied territories. Eyewitness reports of survivors were very scarce. The radio and the newspapers devoted most of their time and space to the relentless war, the struggle to force Nazi Germany into an unconditional surrender. Despite the heavy defeats and the continuing retreat of the German army, all of us refugees from Poland felt very depressed. Prompted by the nagging uncertainty about the fate of my loved ones, I wrote several letters of inquiry to as many individual and official addresses in Lodz as I could think of.

Comrade Verdomitsky arrived from Novosibirsk in the middle of April to take up his new posting. He was a large man in his middle forties, born in Warsaw into a traditional Jewish family that had migrated before the Revolution to Moscow. The new head of the department admitted that he knew very little about railways and that he was very unhappy about being sent to our provincial town, away from his family in Novosibirsk. He then told me that he would be relying on me for the day-to-day running of the department.

I was quite happy about the new set-up. I could continue to do my job without the burden of responsibility. The first favour I asked from my new boss was to give Moyshe a better job. That was not a problem. Moyshe became a train guard for special assignments. He just loved it.

8 May 1945. The horrible war had ended at last, with the complete and humiliating defeat of Nazi Germany. For the first time in history, numerous German cities and their industries had been reduced to rubble. The 'Thousand Year Reich' was finished, its leaders dead or on the run. The following day, the ninth, was declared a public holiday, and a ration of half a litre of vodka per person was issued. The rejoicing of the whole population was genuine, and I got drunk.

Comrade Verdomitsky, the good party man, also had a sharp eye for business. One day, he told me that he might send me to Novosibirsk to present a number of our department's requests to the Ministry of Railways. Winking as he spoke, he added that, while there, I could stay with his family and that I should be able to hand them a few gifts. I understood well what he meant. Lately, the black market had been flooded with good-quality fabrics and clothing, looted by Soviet army personnel in Germany. The soldiers, on their way to the Far East to fight Japan, were selling vast amounts of different merchandise at every railway station where they stopped, and buying vodka with the proceeds. Novosibirsk was an important centre on the Trans-Siberian Railway line, and the local people were making a lot of money, buying up all they could, then reselling it to others, especially to those from the provinces.

I had a word with my mate Moyshe, and he immediately became interested in the projected trip, assuring me that he would be able to sell everything that I could buy. He also advanced the necessary money. Moyshe always seemed to have more money than anybody else. My first trip was very successful, and we made a good profit. I repeated it, and we did even better. Then it was Moyshe's turn to make a couple of successful trips. Comrade Verdomitsky was happy, and, for the first time since I had come to the Soviet Union, I could afford to buy myself some decent clothing.

A registration of Polish citizens wishing to be repatriated to Poland was announced by the authorities in June. At last we had evidence that they would let us leave the Soviet Union. There had always been plenty of sceptics who did not believe that this would happen. With the exception of a very few people, all Polish citizens registered for repatriation by the due date.

I still had had no reply to my letters, and did not hold out much hope for my dear ones. Then, at the beginning of September, I received a very short letter from Fela. The letter had been written in Lodz, at the end of June, and had taken more than two months to reach me. Fela wrote that she had survived the hell of Auschwitz and other camps by a sheer miracle, that she was all alone, and that she would wait for me.

That was the most memorable day of my life. The people around me shared my limitless joy. In the following weeks, I wrote to her every few days, endeavouring to lift her spirits, to inspire her with new hope and optimism for the future, which we would share together, forever. I was the first person in Stalinsk to communicate with a survivor in Lodz. Many refugees in our district, natives of my city of birth, came to see me in search of first-hand news from there.

My mate Moyshe fell in love, and decided to marry the lucky girl — a daughter of Jewish evacuees from the Ukraine — immediately. He would not listen to my argument that it was unfair to take such a step after he had already registered for repatriation as a single man. He reasoned that there would be a shortage of young Jewish women-survivors and he might be unable to find a bride in Poland; that he was nearing forty and could not wait much longer; and that, as I had my betrothed waiting for my return, I was unable to understand him. Moyshe assured me that he was prepared to wait as long as it would take to add his wife's name to his departure documents.

That was his final decision. He wanted me to meet his bride and future in-laws, and other members of their extended family. I was quite impressed. They were all nice people, and they made me feel welcome. The bride was in her late twenties; she was an average sort of person who I thought would probably make a good wife for a fellow like Moyshe. The young couple decided to get their civil marriage certificate in two days' time, and a small celebration was planned for the following evening, in their place. That was in the middle of October. Moyshe moved out from the hostel to the apartment of his in-laws, where the couple was given a separate room. I did not feel comfortable left by myself in the hostel, and I moved into private lodgings soon afterwards.

In the beginning of December, I received the much-awaited letter from Fela. It was long and exhaustive. She wrote about her miraculous survival in more detail, then conveyed the good news that both my sisters had survived and were safe and well, in Sweden. The sad news was that, as I had suspected long before, both my parents, as well as her whole family, had perished. Fela assured me that she was fine and in good health, and that while she was waiting for me she was living in the apartment of a cousin of mine, whom she had got to know in the ghetto after my departure.

It was thanks to that cousin, Szmulek Rozenblum, that she had got my first message, after the liberation. When she accidentally met him on the street in Lodz, he told her that on the noticeboard of the Jewish Community Centre there was a postcard from me, inquiring about her. Fela also mentioned that my good cousin, Fishl Wajnsztok, from whom I had become separated in 1940, had already come back to Lodz.

Although my joy was mixed with sorrow, that letter called for a big celebration. Moyshe invited me to his place for dinner that evening. Everyone around the table shared my happiness, asking a lot of questions and admiring the small picture of Fela that was included in the letter. I had a good cry that night — they were tears of joy.

In the following months, until my departure from Stalinsk, I wrote to Fela often and received many letters from her, all of them addressed to my office. Because the delivery of mail in the Soviet Union was not very efficient, sometimes a number of letters would arrive at the same time. My co-workers at the office worked out a routine in which I had to dance before I was given a letter. As many letters as there were, I had to dance that many times. It was hard work, but it was well worth it.

After January 1946, the repatriation of Polish citizens from different regions of the Soviet Union was intensified. We did not know precisely when our region's turn would come, but our local authorities hinted that it should be in March. I was ready to leave at any time. Not so my mate Moyshe. I sensed a change in his behaviour. He did not seem as happy as previously. My questions were not answered; he would just mumble and drop a word or two about the constant nagging of his wife and her family. The flames of his great love were definitely being extinguished.

When we were officially notified that a train for our repatriation to Poland would be supplied on 19 March, and people began to prepare for the voyage, Moyshe had to tell me the truth. I had been right, he said; he was very unhappy, and his marriage was a big mistake. He had found out a lot of things about his wife's character, and he realised how incompatible the two of them were. He decided to join me for the voyage to Poland by himself, and to leave his wife behind. He would pretend that he was going to Moscow to plead with the central authorities to add her name to his repatriation document. Instead, he would leave home with his luggage and depart with me, with his wife not suspecting anything.

I considered Moyshe's behaviour inhuman, mean, and disgraceful, and I told him so. However, that was his decision. Our promised train was supplied in time. It consisted of about twenty-five freight vans, each fitted out with two tiers of bunks, to accommodate forty people. Food supplies for the whole trip, expected to take four weeks, had to be loaded in Stalinsk. Only fresh bread from local bakeries would be available during stopovers.

A committee of representatives from each van was formed, to supervise the distribution of food, to control hygiene standards, and to maintain order in the whole train during the voyage. Being a 'railway specialist', as well as having had the experience of a few voyages across the Soviet Union in that sort of train, I was elected as representative of our van as soon as I got in.

Moyshe got in the van with me. He stayed inside all the time during the two days of our preparations for departure. Not long before we were to leave, Moyshe's wife came to the railway station to bid me a final goodbye. As she approached our van, Moyshe quickly hid as far as he could under a bunk. She told me that she was not fooled by Moyshe at all. She knew he was deserting her, that he was not going to Moscow, that he would be on the train when it departed. She just wanted to wish me good luck once more, and wanted Moyshe to know that she was not as stupid as he thought.

We departed late on 20 March. The trip was tiring and uneventful. As we approached Poland, I became more excited and impatient. We crossed the border at Przemyśl on 18 April. I had decided long before to leave the train, which was travelling towards the newly acquired Polish territories bordering Germany, and to make my own way to Lodz, as quickly as possible. Before boarding a passenger train going to Cracow, I sent a telegram to Fela from the post office. It cost me a fair amount of money, but the telegram never arrived — the employee evidently pocketed the money. This was my first encounter with the new Polish, Soviet-style bureaucracy.

Moyshe stuck to me like glue and would not let me go by myself — I could not get rid of him. He decided to accompany me to Lodz. He gave me his word that he would leave me alone once we got there. We had been warned to be careful on the trains; anti-Semitism was still alive and well in the new Poland. Jews were being beaten up and murdered in trains, in the cities, and in the shetls. We arrived at Cracow in the evening, and I immediately bought tickets for a train to Lodz, departing at 2.00 a.m. The train was full, but we somehow managed to find seats, and we arrived at the Lodz central railway station at about 6.30 a.m. The address where

Fela was living was some two kilometres from the station. I did not walk, I ran all the way, with Moyshe beside me — he just had to meet Fela before he would leave me.

Chapter Eleven

IT WAS 7.00 a.m., 19 April 1946. I knocked at the door of an apartment, shown to me by the caretaker. My heart was pounding vigorously. The door opened, and there she stood in front of me, my beloved Fela. After a separation of six-and-a-half years, after experiencing hell on earth, she looked more beautiful than ever — a little more mature, and perhaps on the plump side, considering how slim she had been before the war. We fell into each other's arms and stood silently in the hall for a while, as if wanting to make sure that it was not a dream, that we were really together again.

Fela was getting ready to leave for work when I appeared that morning. She had expected me to arrive soon, but she had no idea when. Fela did not go to work that day. There was too much to talk about, there was too much excitement in the house. I met my cousin Szmulek Rozenblum and his young wife, Hanka. I could vaguely remember his father, Yankev (Jacob), who was an uncle of my father. Yankev, a very orthodox Jew who lived with his family in a suburb far from us, on the other side of town, coming to see us on a few occasions before the war. Every time he visited us, he would criticise my father for neglecting my religious education. During my absence, in April 1940, Szmulek's family, along with all the Jewish people of Lodz, had been driven into the ghetto. Afterwards, Szmulek used to visit my family often, and Fela had met him during that time, before she left the ghetto.

Szmulek survived in the Lodz ghetto until he, along with 800 other Jews, was liberated by the Soviet army in January 1945. He had met Fela by chance on the street when she had come back to Lodz, in June. It was Szmulek who had told Fela about my letter on the noticeboard of the Jewish Community Centre. A little later, when she was in desperate need of accommodation, Szmulek came to the rescue. After consulting his wife, Hanka, he found a brass bed in the attic, and invited Fela to move in to their apartment.

While Fela, Shmulek, Hanka, and myself were all talking at the same time, my mate Moyshe stood silent, obviously envious of my good fortune in having found Fela, and relatives as well. After we had breakfast together, Moyshe kept his word. My cousin gave him the address of the Jewish Community Centre for repatriated people, and Moyshe went there, after wishing us good luck.

Fela and I had a lot to talk about, but the one subject we did not touch upon was that of our love. We were both sure about our feelings for each other. We were both longing for the day when we would be together, never to be separated again. I did not need to propose to Fela. I knew that she had waited for me patiently since she had come back to Lodz in June 1945. In that abnormal post-war period, she needed great strength of character and determination just to earn a living and to secure a roof over her head. Unlike a great many Jewish women-survivors, who in their loneliness agreed to marry the first man who offered them some sort of accommodation and keep, Fela, who was a good-looking, intelligent, and bright young woman, had declined all marriage proposals, and had chosen instead to wait for my return from the USSR. It was obvious to both of us that we would get married as soon as possible. It was also a matter of practicality. If we could have been married immediately, it would have simplified our immediate, day-to-day living arrangements at my cousin's place.

Alas, it was not possible. Fela and I wanted a traditional Jewish wedding. I had arrived in the middle of Passover, and, according to Jewish law, no weddings could take place between Passover and Shavuot, the so-called period of mourning. During that period there was just one day, the holiday of Lag B'Omer, when weddings were permitted. But that still meant waiting another month, until 19 May. There was no way out; we had to wait.

Later that day, we sat down and began to discuss our plans for the future. Fela was convinced that we could not remain in Poland for very long. She was disgusted with the continuing anti-Semitic outbursts against the survivors, and did not trust the new communist order at all. She could not forget the hostile reception she and other Jews returning from the camps had encountered from the Polish people, who openly voiced their discontent that too many Jews had survived the Nazi atrocities.

I agreed with her wholeheartedly. There was no future for us in Poland. We would not even consider re-establishing ourselves, striking roots there. We would treat the time we remained there as a temporary stay, as a pause or as an interval, before we would attempt to build a new life and a family in another country. Although both of us were very poor, with no definite prospects for realising our plans, we were optimistic about the future — nothing could stop us after we had found each other again.

Cousin Fishl came over in the evening. We had not seen each other since that day in April 1940 when he had left me in Kizel. That was six years before. Fishl had not changed much — he could not even remember how it had happened. He thought that I had left him. Anyway, he had come back from the Soviet Union some time ago. He did not have a job, but lived not so badly, thanks to his girlfriend, who received money regularly from her relatives in the United States. He'd always been popular with girls, he said as he left.

Before we went to bed, Fela confided in me: she had remained a virgin, through very difficult times, and wished to stay so until our wedding. She knew very well that it meant depriving ourselves of the greatest joy of people in love, for a whole month, but that was how she felt. I understood her very well. Fela was an idealist, a romantic, and a perfectionist. It also had something to do with her Orthodox, puritanical upbringing. She believed in absolute fidelity and in chastity until the wedding. I told her that I would respect her wish; I would just have to wait a little longer. That night, we lay awake for hours, feeling the warmth of each other's bodies, and talking until the early hours of the morning.

Next day, Fela had to go to work. I accompanied her part of the way and then decided to have a look at the city. Lodz had not changed at all, except for the ghetto area, where some streets had been razed and were overgrown with weeds. I felt depressed as I approached the house where our family used to live. It was there, intact; the balcony exactly as it always had been. I went up the stairs and knocked at the door. A woman looked at me through a small opening and shut it quickly when I asked to be let in for a few minutes only. I had enough time to see the large painting above my parents' bed and our coal-stove, still standing in the middle of the room.

I went back to the city centre and walked from street to street, hoping to find a familiar face. I was not very successful, although there were quite a few Jewish people in that area. I was given the address of the Bund premises. It was very close to where I was living. There were a number of people there whom I did not know, but I was immediately recognised and welcomed by a few pre-war comrades and friends. My old mate Bono Wiener, who now had to a leading position in the party, offered to help me find a job in my trade. He also advised me to see him if I needed any financial help. I was very encouraged by the warm reception, but was not convinced by Bono's idea that we should try to rebuild our lives in the new, socialist Poland; that there was a future for a Jewish community in that country.

Our wedding, which took place on 19 May, was a very unusual affair. There were a large number of couples in the same situation as we were in, waiting for Lag B'Omer to get married. It was a conveyor-belt wedding ceremony. As each couple moved under the *chuppah* (canopy), the rabbi quickly recited the service. As soon as he finished, another couple replaced the previous one, and a new ceremony began.

Unlike most of the other couples, we had the good fortune to have some of our relatives at the ceremony, and later at a modest reception, at cousin Szmulek's place. Cousin Fishl and his future wife, Różka, Szmulek and Hanka, and also another cousin, Szmul Leder, who had come to Lodz unexpectedly from Lower Silesia, were present. Fela was given away by her 'guardian angel', Fela Hamer, her saviour in Auschwitz. Fela's husband, Laybl Herszberg, was the best man. Considering the times, we were very lucky.

Since my arrival, Fela had been the provider. She worked in a yarn-spinning factory, and earned just enough money for the two of us. I spent every day looking for a job and for alternative accommodation. We badly needed a place to live in on our own. It was not only the lack of privacy. We thought that we were imposing on the hospitality of my cousin Szmulek and his wife. Finding suitable accommodation was even more difficult than finding a job.

As it happened, both problems were solved at practically the same time. Through a middleman, I found a vacant room: one of four in a large apartment in the centre of the city. There was one catch, though — they demanded 10,000 złoty (about $US250) key-money, which was a huge sum for us. I went to Bono, who promptly asked his treasurer to give me the amount needed. The party had at their disposal moneys received from the Jewish Labour Committee, to help people re-establish themselves.*

We were overjoyed, and moved into our new 'castle' after the wedding. Bono also kept his word to help me get a job. Thanks to his introduction to the chairman of the Polish Socialist Party's large publishing and printing house, I was accepted on their staff as a compositor, in the magazine section. I was very happy to return to my trade. Until we left Lodz, in August 1946, I worked there.

At last we were on our own. At last we could express our feelings in private. Fela and I considered ourselves to be the happiest and luckiest honeymoon couple in the whole world. Our love had conquered all obstacles. We went to work in the mornings, happy that we would earn enough to make a reasonable living. We came home happy to find each other, to be together again, until the next morning. Fela showed herself to be a terrific homemaker, too. The single room we occupied was transformed by her into a warm home, where relatives and friends often visited us.

At that time, my two sisters were living in Norrköping, in central Sweden. In August 1944, when the Germans decided to liquidate the Lodz ghetto, they, along with all the inhabitants, were loaded into grossly overcrowded railway

---

* The Jewish Labor Committee was an American Jewish trade union organisation with Bundist links that still exists today. It supported survivors in post-war Poland.

trucks and transported to Auschwitz. One day, Fela, an old inmate of that notorious camp, learned from a friend that both my sisters had been spotted among the new arrivals. Fela had not seen them since her departure from Lodz on April 1941, and was anxious to talk to them. Risking heavy punishment for disobeying a camp rule that forbade inmates from having any contacts with new arrivals, Fela managed to meet them and was able to talk to them.

My sisters were lucky. They were kept in Auschwitz for one week only, before they were moved, together, to a labour camp near Berlin. The conditions in that camp were not as bad as in others, and they worked in a Krupp ammunition factory until mid-April 1945. At that time, Count Bernadotte of the Swedish Red Cross obtained permission from the infamous Heinrich Himmler to evacuate 10,000 sick inmates, mostly women, from German concentration and labour camps. The names of my two sisters were among those in the lists of evacuees. The chosen inmates were taken to an assembly point, the Ravensbrück camp.

What followed was a perilous journey by buses and trains across Germany and Denmark. At one stage, they were strafed by Allied aircraft, who suspected the convoy was carrying German army units under the camouflage of Red Cross flags. There were many casualties among the evacuees. However, my sisters' convoy arrived safely in Sweden on 28 April after crossing the sea in open barges.

On arrival, the sick people were immediately hospitalised, but a substantial number of them were in such poor physical condition that their lives could not be saved. (In 1977, when

Fela and I visited my sister in Norrköping, she showed us numerous graves of young people at the cemetery — they had all died soon after their arrival in 1945.) The other evacuees, although weak and emaciated, were nurtured back to health in special reception centres set up by the Swedish government all over the country. My two sisters were sent to a place near Norrköping, about 160 kilometres south-west of Stockholm. When they regained their strength and were fit for work, they were given jobs in a local textile factory, obtained accommodation, and stayed in that city.

I wrote to them as soon as I reached Lodz. They were overjoyed by my safe return, and more so by the fact that Fela and I were reunited. They themselves were not too prosperous, but they tried to help us as much as they could. For a time, we even considered joining them in Sweden. However, the officials at the Swedish embassy in Poland were not willing to issue the necessary travel documents to us. We had to give up that idea for the time being.

The Bund party premises, in the centre of the city, were a good meeting point. Every time I went there, there was a chance I would meet old acquaintances or friends who had just arrived from the Soviet Union or from somewhere else. In that period, Lodz, not Warsaw, which was still in ruins, was the centre of all the Jewish communities of Poland. A conference of all party branches was organised at the end of May. Delegates from all over the country had arrived in Lodz. Among them, coming from Lower Silesia, were my schoolmates Zishe Zamieczkowski and Chil Infeld. All of us were overjoyed — we had not heard from each other since 1939. They came to visit us, and met Fela. They were all married, and had spent the war years in the Soviet Union.

The conference was a very interesting affair. It had before it a motion of the executive, supported by the central committee in New York, that the party fully commit to the rebuilding of Jewish communities in the new Polish Republic, and that, in partnership with the Polish Socialist Party, the Bund take part in the political transformation of the country into a socialist society.

Heated debates went on for two days. Opposing the motion, speaker after speaker pointed out that Poland was like a cemetery; that deep-seated, pathological anti-Semitism was rampant in all sections of Polish society; that Jews were still and would remain in peril in Poland; that we could not trust the communists to allow the existence of any party but their own; that all activities of the Bund in Poland should be regarded as temporary; and, finally, that the resources of the party should be utilised to organise and help the orderly emigration of comrades and their families.

I fully supported the opposition, and could not understand the supporters of the motion. To me, they seemed like the proverbial 'none so blind as those who do not want to see'. They put on blinkers, and were happy to follow the old dogmas. The result was a foregone conclusion: the motion of the executive was passed, although not with a large majority.

Two events in the following two months virtually destroyed the arguments of the majority. In June, a well-known party member, Fishke Najman, an army officer in active service, was bludgeoned to death in his own apartment by unknown thugs. A large mass of people, party members, and others, as well as army colleagues, attended the funeral. Despite the uplifting speeches at the graveside, all the Jewish mourners were terribly depressed by that brutal, murderous act.

Then, in July, news came of a horrible pogrom in Kielce, a medium-sized city in Poland. It was like in the czarist times. Forty-two Jews, including children, were killed, and dozens injured, by a mob of over 1,000 rioting Poles. Under the pretext of the medieval blood libel, a rumour that Jews had murdered a Christian boy had spread in the previous days. During the well-organised riot, which had been instigated by the local police, the mob systematically broke into Jewish homes, beating and killing the inhabitants. No one intervened — not the church, nor the police, nor the army. After the Kielce pogrom, it should have been clear to everyone that there was no room for Jews in Poland. Not so to the Bund leadership; they were still not convinced.

The Jewish community was panic-stricken. The hitherto steady flow of illegal departures from Poland became a flood. The *Bricha*, an underground organisation consisting of former partisans, veterans of the Jewish Brigade from Palestine that had served with the British army in Europe, and envoys from Palestine, began to ferry thousands of Jews daily across frontiers — ostensibly illegally, but with the wholehearted support of the Polish and other governments. Their destinations were the DP (Displaced Persons') camps in West Germany, Austria, and Italy. The world Zionist leadership, who was behind the operation, hoped that the majority of these people would proceed from there to Palestine. In the three months following the Kielce pogrom, about 70,000 Jews, most of whom had survived the war in the Soviet Union, left Poland.

We, too, decided that we could not remain in Poland for much longer. We wanted Szmulek and Hanka to join us, but they hesitated because Hanka was pregnant. Fishl Wajnsztok and his wife left in July, and we too began to prepare for departure. There were a few practical items to attend to before we could leave. We had to sell anything we could, quickly, to build up some capital. Our first task was to find a buyer for our apartment — that was our main asset — but it had to be done quietly, as taking key-money was illegal at the time. I also wanted to draw my full severance entitlements from my workplace. Fela had no such problems with her employer, a Jew, who just wished her good luck.

In the first week of August, we were ready. We had sold everything we could. When I told the director of my firm that I was just changing jobs, he immediately understood the truth, and asked me if I could sell him my apartment, which he needed for a new arrival. He did not haggle and paid the full amount asked, on the spot.

On the day of our departure, we went to take our leave of Szmulek and Hanka. We were genuinely fond of them, and parting with them made us sad. In those uncertain times, it was impossible to foresee when we would see them again. We kept in touch with them through the years. After our departure, Hanka gave birth to a son, Yankl, and then another, Marek (Yossi). Later, Szmulek had some problems with the authorities and fled Poland illegally, by himself. Initially, he settled in West Germany, where Hanka, who had had a very tough time on her own in Poland, was able to join him, and they had a third son, Dovid. The family later moved to Antwerp, Belgium, where the sons could receive an Orthodox religious education. Szmulek himself continued to conduct his business in Frankfurt.

It was not until January 1973 that we managed to visit them, after a trip to Israel and France. By that time, their oldest son, Yankl, was already married, and adhered to a strict religious lifestyle, as did his parents and in-laws. The second son, Marek, had just began a medical course at a university, and the youngest one, Dovid, was a *bar-mitzvah* boy. It was a great joy to see Hanka and Szmulek after more than twenty-six years. We spent five happy days with them, and got to know their sons.

In 1976, we received a letter from Szmulek telling us that Hanka had died suddenly. She had entered hospital for a routine operation, but complications had developed after surgery. She was only fifty years old. Szmulek was devastated. We visited him again a year later, in 1977. The family was well. He had grandchildren, Marek was doing well at university, and Dovid was growing into a fine young man. Szmulek, however, was a different person. He was inconsolable.

As the years passed, we always wrote to each other. Marek became a successful doctor. He married, and his wife gave birth to twin boys. Dovid, too, had married, in the United States, where he was studying. The last time we saw Szmulek was in the summer of 1990. He came to visit us in Zurich, where we were staying, after a trip to Israel and France. He has never remarried.[**]

I went to the Bund premises by myself. When I told Bono that we would be leaving in a few hours' time, he was greatly disappointed. His exact words were: 'You too, Fishl, are deserting the battleground. It is here where we must stay and fight for our ideals, now that we have a chance to build a socialist society.' My answer was simple: 'It is not our battle; this ground is poisoned, and this society is completely rotten. It will never change.'

The next time I saw Bono was in November 1947, in Paris. He had attended the first world conference of Bundist organisations in Brussels in May, and had come to address a meeting of the Paris organisation. He was still full of fight, still defending his viewpoint of remaining and working in Poland.

On our arrival in Melbourne, in January 1952, Bono greeted me at the Kadimah, Melbourne's Jewish cultural centre. He had had to flee Poland in 1948 in haste, after all political parties, apart from the communists, were declared illegal. He had had to organise a network of smugglers in a hurry, to help those party members who were ready to travel

---

[**] Szmulek joined his children in Antwerp, where he died in 2014. He never did remarry.

at short notice to cross the border. Left behind were many who, for personal or family reasons, could not undertake the risky journey at that time. I repeated to Bono the words that he had said to me on the day of my departure from Lodz. Bono, however, always had a ready answer. He still thought that he had been right at the time.

Chapter Twelve

THE TRAIN TRIP to Kłodzko, on the Czechoslovak border, was uneventful, and we arrived there in the evening. We were with a group of about 200 people: men, women, and children, led by a few tough-looking men. Overnight, we stayed in a large building and slept on the bare boards of a table. During the day, the command to march was given, and we simply walked through a border point, with the Polish guards just standing there and smiling. It was evident that they had received a hefty bribe.

We were already in Czechoslovakia, and we quickly marched towards a large compound, encircled by barbed wire. We spent the night there, and the next morning we boarded a train that travelled, unhindered, through Bratislava into the Soviet-occupied part of Austria, then to Vienna, and from there to a Displaced Persons' camp in Linz, in the American zone. The Linz camp served as a temporary holding point for new arrivals before their departure to the DP camps in the American zone of Germany.

Our stay in Linz was longer than usual. Due to the large number of people arriving there daily, the German authorities could not keep up with the organisation and preparation of new camps. In Linz, we were looked after comparatively well, but we were impatient to move on, to Germany. Towards the end of August, we boarded a train and travelled to Landshut, a small town in Bavaria. There were thousands of people there, accommodated in military tents, waiting for transportation to their designated camps.

After spending a few days and nights there, we decided that the time for action had come. Fela had the address of her camp girlfriend Fredzia, who lived in the small town of Erding, near Munich. Fela went there alone, to meet her and her husband, as well as to have a look around. When Fela came back, unsure of what we should do, I went to Feldafing, a large camp on the other side of Munich, from where the Bund was co-ordinating its activities in all camps. I hoped that they could quickly find us a DP camp, but I was not successful — there were just too many people arriving at the same time.

On my return, Fela and I agreed to accept her girlfriend's invitation to stay with them for a few days. The nights were getting colder, the tents were very uncomfortable, and there was a general lack of facilities for personal hygiene. We did not have to check-out with anyone — we were free to leave. We packed our belongings and boarded a train to Munich, then to Erding.

Fredzia and her husband, Genek, received us very well. Erding was a lovely medieval township, and we spent a pleasurable week there. As for the immediate future, we agreed to join a kibbutz that occupied a farm near Erding and was preparing its members to settle on the land in Palestine. The leader of the kibbutz was a friend of Genek, and he well understood that we would not stay with them, that we just needed a temporary home. As a matter of fact, we stayed with them until the end of September, and we enjoyed every minute of it. It was a new experience for us.

There were lots of young, pleasant people around; the camaraderie was great. We worked in the fields during the days, and in the evenings we had a lot of fun, learning Hebrew songs and dances.

My cousin Fishl and his wife, Różka, lived in a camp in the small town of Velmeden, near Kassel, in the state of Hessen. He wrote to us, insisting that we join them there — temporarily at least. We thought about it for a while, then accepted their offer. At the beginning of October, we left the kibbutz and travelled north to Frankfurt, Kassel, and then to Velmeden. The camp was housed in what had been the barracks of the Luftwaffe, on the crest of a decent hill. It looked very picturesque, as did the whole township, but climbing the steep hill was quite strenuous.

Fishl and Różka received us with open arms. They were pleased to see us, and put up an extra bed in the small room they occupied. We were registered to receive rations immediately. It was a small camp, housing a few hundred people only — one of a number of smaller camps in the district, which were treated and managed as one unit. Różka worked in the camp kitchen, and Fishl with the camp police. The DPs were provided for by the UNRRA (United Nations

Relief and Rehabilitation Administration) and the Joint (American Jewish Joint Distribution Committee). Each DP received his or her basic entitlement, which was really not enough. Each camp was autonomous. It had its own management, administration, police, and other departments, which ran kitchens and all other necessary services, for the, in many places, huge communities. A large percentage of people in the camps were employed to fulfil all these duties. In lieu of pay, they received Joint parcels, which contained, among other things, the most sought-after means of exchange: cigarettes and coffee.

Fela and I were not too happy with the living arrangements. It was too cramped, and I was looking for different work. Not far from Velmeden, in the town of Eschwege, there was a large camp that published its own weekly newspaper, as did a number of other camps. I also knew that a number of Bundists had settled there. About a week after our arrival at Velmeden, I went there, alone. As soon as I entered the camp office and told them that I was a compositor, they would not let me go. It just happened that they badly wanted to change their paper to Yiddish type, instead of the previously used Latin, and were desperate to find a man who could organise and run a typesetting shop. They promised to look after me well and to help me settle in, but wanted me to start immediately. I agreed to come within a few days.

Before I left, I met the leader of the Bund group, who held a responsible position in the camp administration. He welcomed me warmly and was very happy that I was going to join the group. Fela was delighted with the turn of events. Fishl and Różka were happy, too. Two days later, we came to Eschwege.

I had made a good decision. We found a few pre-war friends in Eschwege, and the Bund group greeted us with open arms. Although our first accommodation was not the best, I was promised a separate room in the building where the typesetting shop was being set up. The newspaper editor asked me to come with him to Frankfurt, where I chose the necessary Yiddish type fonts from the famous Stempel type foundry. They had just started to produce them, from their old Hebrew matrices, which they had hidden during the Nazi era. All our purchases were paid for in coffee and cigarettes.

Back in Eschwege, I rolled up my sleeves and got to work. I was given carpenters, electricians, and plumbers to set up the room. From our German printer in town, I brought back a truckload of type cabinets, type cases, galleys, spacing materials, and all the other necessary odds and ends. Within days, everything was ready.

They somehow found another compositor, too, and we both got to work, producing an eight-page tabloid, all handset, for the following edition. We worked long hours every day in order to meet the deadline. When the first Yiddish newspaper appeared in Eschwege, it was a special occasion. Everybody congratulated us on a fine effort. For the next edition, our workload was lightened with the employment of a third compositor. From then on, publishing the weekly became routine.

We were happy. I enjoyed my work, and Fela was busy arranging our new home — a room on our own. The winter had set in and it was bitterly cold, but we had all the coal we needed from the well-supplied typesetting room, which was next door to where we lived. The Bund group was active, and I was chosen as secretary. We had regular meetings and, from time to time, small celebrations. The main task of the executive was to co-ordinate the migration opportunities of comrades to different countries. That required keeping in regular communication with the headquarters in Feldafing, and with overseas organisations as well.

Towards the end of January, Fela told me that she thought she was pregnant. She was definite about not wanting to give birth to our child on German soil. We had to find a place to emigrate to, soon. I had previously applied to the Swedish embassy for an entry permit to Sweden. We could not understand why they had refused us, since they issued permits to other DPs. I also tried to contact my American relatives by placing an advertisement in the New York *Forverts* Yiddish daily. Not long afterwards, I received a letter from my oldest uncle, Julius. He wrote that he had already retired, that he was a pensioner, and that the only person who could and should help me was uncle Max, in Chicago. At the time, when Fela told me the happy news, I was waiting for a reply to my plea for help from uncle Max.

We did not have to wait too long. A letter arrived soon, written on the official letterhead of a law firm, by a person who was supposed to be the spokesman for my uncle Max. Instead of being offered help, I was given a lecture. I was told that we did not deserve any different treatment than other Jewish survivors in Europe, who were being cared for by American Jewish welfare agencies, the recipients of my relatives' generous financial support. The writer then reminded me that they, the American Jews, had also suffered a lot in World War II. They had enlisted in their army, they had fought the Japanese and the Germans, and they had lost a great number of men. I felt offended and humiliated. Until 1980, I had no contact with any of my American relatives.

(Eventually, we did meet them, in June 1982. Cousin Arthur, Max's son, who had visited us Melbourne in 1981, invited us and my sisters, Rose and Maria, to Chicago. At a special reunion lunch at his place, we met three generations of Rosenblums (as they spelt their surname), including seven first cousins and an uncle. We all felt excited and genuinely happy — our lives suddenly enriched. We forgave all of them everything that had happened in the past. So much did we enjoy their company that we came again in 1987 and 1992.)

Fela was pregnant all right. She looked exceptionally well, and had a terrific appetite. She also had a great craving for apples. Luckily, they were obtainable on the black market. The whole of West Germany was one great black market at that time, and the DP camps were no exception. Everything was obtainable in the camp, at the right price. I was able to buy a whole box of good-quality apples at a time — Fela was never short of apples. It was a very happy time for both of us, despite the difficulties of finding a country that would let us in.

A two-day conference of Bundist groups in West Germany was called for the last week in February, in Munich. I was sent there as one of three Eschwege delegates. It meant quite a long trip for us. The delegates were promised accommodation in nearby Feldafing. The conference was a good occasion to meet old friends. In fact, there were a number of my old schoolmates and classmates present. Among them was Laye Grundman and her husband, Moyshe Ajzenbud, whom I met there for the first time.

The main topic of the conference was emigration, and it was interesting enough. We heard first-hand reports of current and future opportunities for settling in different countries. At the end of official business, some announcements were made. Among them was a request from *Undzer Shtime* (*Our Voice*), the Bundist daily newspaper in Paris, for a compositor willing to move to Paris immediately. They offered to pay for the trip, and guaranteed a permanent job. Without hesitation, I accepted the offer. We had no relatives or friends in Paris, but I knew that Fela was desperate to leave Germany. I had only one condition: if my cousin and his wife wanted to come with us, they, too, should be accepted for the trip to Paris. My condition was agreed to.

I felt a little uneasy, having made such an important decision without consulting Fela. In fact, the trip to Paris, (without proper travel documents, but led by an experienced smuggler who had been taking groups of Bundists and sympathisers from West Germany to Paris on a regular basis), was scheduled to leave in about two days' time. I had to travel to Eschwege to fetch Fela, then to Velmeden to see

Fishl and Różka, and then had to return to Feldafing.

When I came home the following morning, after an all-night train trip, and asked Fela if she would like us to settle in Paris, she was delighted. I told her we would have to leave within two hours, but she was packed and ready before then. On the way out, we said goodbye to our friends and to the newspaper editor. We caught the train to Velmeden, and offered Fishl and Różka the chance to come with us to Paris.

They both hesitated. They feared the unknown. In Velmeden, they had their own room and they had enough food, they said. It was all right for us — I had been guaranteed a job. But Fishl, who had no trade qualifications, how would he earn a living, and how would they find accommodation? Unfortunately, I could not answer their questions. I just thought it would be nice to have relatives living close-by — we could help each other, and we would feel less lonely in a new country. They declined our proposition, and we made the journey to Feldafing by ourselves.

The next time we met Fishl and Różka was nearly twenty-two years later, on our first trip to Israel in late December 1968. They had arrived there at the beginning of 1949, after the establishment of the Jewish state, and settled in Haifa, where their only daughter, Sarah, was born.

We spent a night in Feldafing, then the next morning we went to Munich and boarded a train to Strasbourg. We were with a group of about forty people who had paid $50 each for the trip. Among them was Różka (Rose) Goldblum, whom I knew from school and from Skif in Lodz. It was a fast train, and we had a very pleasant trip. In the evening, when we arrived in Strasbourg, already on French soil, we were all in a good mood. Previously, we had stopped at the border, but were not bothered at all by the guards and customs people, who obviously had a longstanding agreement with our smuggler. After a short wait, we changed trains and proceeded to Paris. We stepped down at Gare de l'Est on the morning of 2 March 1947.

Chapter Thirteen

'THE CITY OF LIGHTS', Paris, greeted us with spring sunshine as Mademoiselle Solange, the representative of the Bund-affiliated *Arbeter Ring* (Workers' Circle) cultural organisation, escorted us to their premises, which also housed the local Bund organisation, as well as their restaurant. After we were served a meal, on the house, some people among our group left with waiting relatives. The rest of us needed help in finding accommodation and in settling some legal matters associated with our arrival.

That afternoon, Mademoiselle Solange went with us to the Prefecture of Police. It took the whole afternoon to register each of us as stateless, illegal entrants to the country, and we were issued with official three-month permits of residence. (At that time, the immigration laws of France had a loophole: once a person entered the country, no matter how, that person could not be deported, unless he or she committed a crime. A large number of Jewish people from eastern Europe used that loophole either to settle in France or to use it as a transit point for their final destination.) Armed with the permit of residence, I was able to obtain a work permit from the Ministry of Labour a couple of days later.

In the years to come, those periodic visits to the prefecture to renew the permit of residence, as well as to the Ministry of Labour to renew the work permit, were the least-pleasant experiences in the life of a migrant in France. Each of those visits meant the loss of at least half a day. It was not only time-consuming; it was also demeaning. The bureaucrats handling the usually large number of waiting people were heartless, rude, and in some instances offensive — treating each applicant as an adversary.

Back at the *Arbeter Ring*, I was greeted by the administrator of *Undzer Shtime*, who informed me that a general strike of all newspaper offices in Paris had begun during the previous week. He assured me, however, that I would be paid enough to live on for the duration of the strike. After spending the first night in a terrible hotel room without windows, we were helped the next day to find decent hotel accommodation. Near the Gare de Lyon, it consisted of only one room, but Fela transformed it in no time into a real home. She was a master at improvisation. Instead of a kitchen, she used a Primus kerosene stove, which had been urgently dispatched to us from Sweden by my sister Ruchl. Our table was always covered with a cloth, and she kept the room spotlessly clean. We even entertained visitors there — a few pre-war acquaintances, as well as some new friends, mostly Bundists.

As soon as we settled down in our new 'palace', Fela went for her first pre-natal check-up, and was found to be in excellent shape. After the newspaper strike ended, I could at last start working at the Bundist daily. The job proved to be not a hard one. In no time, I became very friendly with my workmates. The editor and his colleagues were leaders of the local party branch, and I enjoyed rubbing shoulders and working with them every day. It was a very happy workplace, and I earned good money there — enough to cover all our living expenses.

The six-month period between our arrival in Paris and the birth of our son was one of the happiest in our lives. For the first time, Fela and I found ourselves in a free, Western country, in a beautiful city that allowed us to make up for the years of our youth, cruelly interrupted by the war. It was also our real honeymoon, since we had had neither the money nor the opportunity to have one before. I worked a permanent afternoon shift, between 3.30 and 11.00 p.m., and we used all our free time to explore Paris. We fell in love with that city, and enjoyed every minute.

From the very beginning, even without knowing the language, I moved around the huge city easily, thanks to its excellent underground rail system, the Metro. As soon as it was possible, I enrolled in the Alliance Francaise school, to learn French. Fela attended French-language courses at the *Arbeter Ring*. It was not an easy language for us to learn, but we both made very good and speedy progress. At that time, Fela also had the good fortune to get in touch with one of her camp sisters, Regina Besserman, who had settled in Paris right after the war. Regina was already married and was also expecting her first child. Regina and Fela became very good friends; it was a friendship that would last until Regina's death in 1991.

As the time of our baby's birth approached, we were desperate to find an apartment. Eventually, Fela heard of a small ground-floor apartment, available in the outer suburb of Clichy. Again, as previously in Lodz, we had to pay key-money, which we did not possess. We were helped by the *Arbeter Ring*. They had special American funds available for helping new arrivals to re-establish themselves. They did not ask too many questions, and handed me the sum needed. A month before the baby was due, we moved in to our first, two-room apartment. It was not much of a place, but we had no option — we could not stay in the hotel room with a baby. We somehow managed to procure the essential furniture, I put a new coat of paint on the walls and ceilings, and our new home did not look too bad at all.

Fela entered the Rothschild hospital on 18 September 1947. She had an exceptionally difficult time before she gave birth to our son on the following day, 19 September. We named him Henri (Henry), as a French equivalent to the name of Fela's father, Chil (Yechiel), which in turn became Henri's Jewish name. He was a beautiful, healthy baby, and we were the proudest parents when we took him home.

During that time and in the following weeks, we felt acutely our lack of relatives. As soon as she came home, Fela developed an abscess on her breast and could not feed the baby. A substitute of suitable milk powder had to be found, and that did not prove to be easy. As well, the doctor treating Fela prescribed the new anti-infection drug Penicillin, which had to be injected every four hours, day and night. The visiting nurse, who was hired to make those injections during the next few days, insisted that I accompany her from her home to us and back, at night-time. To make matters worse, I could not take any time off from work, since it was a daily newspaper and there was no one to replace me. We all had a pretty hard time — Fela, the baby, and myself. Slowly, Fela got better, and a perfect formula for our baby's bottle was found. Fela's greatest regret, though, was not being able to breast-feed her first-born.

Things were looking up. Fela got well, and our son was gaining weight and strength rapidly. At six months, he stood up in his cot; at nine months, he began to walk. Our circle of friends widened appreciably, and we also got to know a few good neighbours. Regina Besserman was very helpful during Fela's sickness, and afterwards, too. Fela also became very friendly with a young Jewish woman from Cracow who lived with her husband and young son not far from us. People used to visit us often, and we reciprocated. It was no problem at all to take the baby in his pram into the Metro — no matter where our friends lived, we could travel anywhere in Paris.

In the summer of 1948, I booked a room in a holiday house in Le Tréport, Normandy, for two months. Fela and the baby stayed there the whole time. I spent the two weeks of my annual leave there, and the weekends, from Saturday morning until Sunday afternoon. That was our first holiday. We enjoyed the lovely fishing village, its friendly people, and the beautiful seashore.

After the United Nations voted for the partition of Palestine on 29 November 1947, the Bund in Paris was embroiled in a bitter internal division about its attitude towards the establishment of a Jewish state. The hard-liners — the dogmatic anti-Zionists, socialists, and internationalists — claimed that the party should stick to its old approach: that the creation of a Jewish state could not and would not solve the problems of the Jewish people. Wherever Jews lived, they would have to participate in the struggle for socialism, the attainment of which would usher in a new era for all mankind, including Jews. According to them, the small Jewish state, of doubtful economic viability, would remain only one of the worldwide Jewish communities, which would still need to apply all their resources towards their own needs.

Opposing that view were a considerable number of members, long established in France, as well as recently settled. Their main argument was that the party could not take a stand that was diametrically opposed to the wishes and aspirations of the absolute majority of the Jewish people, who for nearly 2,000 years had dreamed of and yearned for the re-establishment of their state. In addition, they argued, we should have learned a lesson from the recent catastrophe, when Jews in Europe were left to their terrible fate by the peoples of the world — no country had offered them a refuge, even when it was still possible to leave Nazi Germany or the occupied territories. The existence of a Jewish state would certainly assure a safe haven for Jews, should they need one in the future. I supported this view.

Heated discussions went on in the party and in its newspaper, until the State of Israel was proclaimed in Tel Aviv. On the afternoon of 14 May, we were preparing the next morning's edition of the paper, as usual. Page one was normally kept open for late news. There were two compositors on the staff, but only one was needed for the closing-up of page one. Each evening, one of us was able to leave work early.

On that particular evening, it was my turn to stay on. The editor working with me was David Anin, a native of Riga: a true intellectual and an excellent journalist. The page-one lead story was already in place. Under the heading: 'The State of Israel Proclaimed', it reported, word for word, David Ben-Gurion's speech, which had been received by telegraph, as well as presenting reports of the tense situation in Israel on the eve of its independence. There was other general local and world news on the page. At the bottom, Mr Anin had put in an item about the pending arrival in Paris of Princess Elizabeth and Prince Phillip, including a photograph of the couple.

At about 10.00 p.m., the chief editor, Alexandre Minc, a Trotskyite in the not-too-distant past, showed up to be present at the closing-up of the edition, as was his habit. He had one glance at the lead story and became enraged. He had a terrible argument with Mr Anin. He yelled that by the time our newspaper reached its readers the Jewish state could be already gone, defeated by the combined might of the Arab armies, who at this very moment were already attacking it from every direction. Mr Minc told Mr Anin to take an early night, took off his coat, and asked me to rearrange the page. Princess Elizabeth's visit became the lead story, splashed over five columns, with a little more text around the photograph. The proclamation of the State of Israel, together with accompanying news items, was moved to the bottom corner of the page. I did what he asked me to do — I had no option — but I felt ashamed of my contribution to an act of political stupidity and pig-headed dogma.

As Mr Minc predicted, Israel was attacked by all the Arab armies, and was fighting for her survival. But she was not yet defeated. On the contrary, her army did well in the battles. In common with all the Jewish communities in the world, the Jews of France were united in their support for the fledgling state. Large sums of money were raised, all sorts of material support was planned, and lots of young men volunteered to fight in the Israeli army. Facing such a situation, the Bund organisation had to decide its attitude quickly: could they, as a party, stand apart and not support the Jews of Israel, who were fighting for their very survival? Even the Jewish communists, who were influential in France, loudly supported Israel.

There was no doubt that the majority of Bundists offered their help as individuals. However, that was not enough. In order to remain viable in the Jewish community, the party had to make a whole-hearted, open, and unqualified declaration of support for Israel in her hour of need. An extraordinary meeting of the party was called to discuss this issue. After lengthy deliberations, a resolution of support for Israel was moved and passed. The opponents of the resolution, Mr Minc and his cronies, would not give in. They raised several objections to the publication of the resolution, the most important being that we were obliged to consult the co-ordinating committee of the Bund in New York before such a fundamental ideological move could be made.

Within a week, the Bund's chief theoretician and editor of the *Undzer Tsayt* (*Our Time*) party magazine, Mr Emanuel Scherer, arrived from New York, and an urgent meeting was called. The issue of support for Israel was again debated until midnight, and a supplementary meeting had to be called for the following evening. Mr Scherer insisted that we had no right to change the party line, and that he would not leave until the original resolution was revoked. He acknowledged the right of members to support Israel in any way they wanted to, as individuals; the Paris organisation, however, could not — we had no right to change the party line. The opponents of the resolution won, but the Bund became more marginalised than ever in Jewish communities all over the world. Myself, I more and more doubted the whole philosophy of the party.

In the autumn of 1948, our newspaper began to experience financial difficulties. The subsidies from America as well as the advertising revenue had shrunk, and the circulation had dropped considerably. In order to cut costs, the administration decided to change the paper from a broadsheet to a tabloid, retaining the same number of pages. There was really not enough work for two compositors. For a while we tried to share the job and the income, but it just was not possible for two families to live off one job. Since I had come last onto the staff, I decided to look for another job.

There were two more Yiddish dailies in Paris, the Zionist *Undzer Vort* (*Our Word*) and the communist *Naye Prese* (*New Press*), but they had no vacancies for a compositor. However, the Zionist daily owned a commercial printing company, too, and they offered me a job in their magazine department. My knowledge of the French language was so good that they did not question my ability to handle the work, which was only in French. I was happy to have found a better-paying job, and to broaden my experience in the trade as well.

However, we were very unhappy with our apartment — not just because it was too small, but because there were large patches of dampness on the walls. As winter approached, we worried about the possible health risk this posed to our son. Then we had a stroke of good fortune. One of our neighbours, who lived with his wife in an apartment on the first floor, offered us his apartment. They were childless, and had taken a liking to us and our little boy. The couple operated a hairdressing salon at the street level of the building, and intended to move into the apartment above their salon. We were overjoyed by their kindness, and immediately arranged for an official transfer at the landlord's office. Towards the end of 1948, we moved into our new, much larger apartment. We felt on top of the world, and acquired more furniture and household goods. We were determined to strike roots in France, our adopted country, which we had liked from the very first day

I was doing well in my new job, too. Although the

business was owned by the Zionist daily, it was operated independently as a commercial printing company, called Avouka, and managed by a Mr Eidess, a Latvian Jew, who had settled in France in the 1920s. There were fifteen people employed on the factory floor: five compositors, eight machinists, and two apprentices. The bulk of the production, all by letterpress, consisted of magazines for trade unions, cultural organisations, and nudists.

A few weeks after I started, Mr Eidess invited me upstairs to his office. At first we had an informal, friendly talk. He asked a number of personal questions about myself, my family, and our wartime experiences. He was a man in his late forties, with a grown-up family. They had all survived in France, in the Free Zone. Turning to business, Mr Eidess confided in me that he should have been spending most of his time servicing existing clients and chasing new ones. Instead, he had to spend whole days in the factory, supervising routine work, because production usually lagged behind, and deliveries were seldom made on time. He said that he was dissatisfied with his foreman, who simply did not perform. He thought that, although it would be a challenge for me, I could do a much better job running the place, despite my lack of experience in French printing firms. Mr Eidess than offered me the job, which carried a much better salary as well. I hesitated a little, but, after consulting Fela, I accepted the challenge.

Our family was very happy during the first three months of 1949. We settled well in our new apartment. Fela stayed home with our little boy, who was admired by all our neighbours and friends. He already spoke French and Yiddish, and knew precisely which language to use with different people. I was successful in my new position at Avouka, and earned much more money than I had previously — enough for a good living for the three of us. Working all day with French-speaking people helped me to continually improve my knowledge of that language. For the first time since our arrival in France, I worked normal hours. Except for rare occasions, I had whole weekends free, and could enjoy them with the family.

At that time, life in France was never dull. Politically, it was like a boiling cauldron. As the cold war raged in Europe, the three major parties in France were the communists, the socialists, and the Christian Democrats, known as the MRP. However, there were also a number of smaller, long-established parties. Due to the French proportional representation electoral system, no party could ever form a government on its own — it could only be formed in coalition with one or a number of other parties. Consequently, governments were unstable and usually broke up after a few months. A political crisis would follow until a new coalition could be stitched together to form a new government, which would last for a while. Invariably, the ensuing internal bickering would lead to another break-up.

In April 1949, Fela became seriously ill. Her gall bladder had virtually stopped functioning as a consequence of the long periods of hunger she had endured and the dreadful food she had had to eat in the Lodz ghetto and in the

German camps during the war years. She had one painful attack after another, and at the end of the month was affected with jaundice, too. Her doctor decided that she had to be hospitalised immediately.

Since we had no one to look after Henri, I was desperate to find a place where he would be taken care of during his mother's illness. Someone gave me the address of a French family who lived about thirty kilometres from Paris. I went there with my little boy. They seemed to be an ordinary couple who were making a living by caring for young children. They were willing to take in Henri, for an agreed weekly sum. It was heart-breaking to leave him there, among strangers, but we had no alternative.

In hospital, Fela underwent a number of tests. Her condition did not improve, and she lost a lot of weight. On top of her illness, she was very worried about Henri. Every time I went to see her, I had to lie to her, saying that our son was being well looked after. In fact, he was miserable. I used to visit him every Saturday. As soon as he saw me, he would begin to cry and would not stop. I sensed that he was hungry, too — whatever I brought him to eat he would gobble up in no time. Parting with him was the hardest thing — no matter what I told him or promised him, he would not let me go.

After six weeks, the doctors treating Fela at the hospital admitted that they could not diagnose the exact cause of her gall-bladder malfunction. They proposed to operate on her to find out what the problem was. Fela decided against it — she did not trust them at all. She knew that some patients in her ward had died on the operating table. Surgery of the gall bladder was not very successful at that time, and she was afraid that her little boy would be motherless. She could not bear the separation from her son any longer, and insisted on being discharged, against the doctor's advice. I took her home, then went to fetch Henri.

Fela became extremely sad when she realised that her little boy did not recognise her. When she wanted to take him in her arms, he struggled and cried. He clung to me and did not let me go to work. He ate all day long, and kept asking for more. Fela made up her mind: in order not to be separated from her son again, she simply had to get well. Through the combination of a strict diet and strong willpower, her health improved to such a degree that she regained her strength and the lost weight within a comparatively short time. It took Henri just a few days to get used to his mother again. He quickly forgot the terrible nightmare he had gone through during his mother's illness. His laughter and constant chatter played no small role in restoring Fela's health. As the summer progressed, life in our household was back to normal again — full of happiness and love.

Chapter Fourteen

TWO IMPORTANT EVENTS occurred in the beginning of 1950. The first was a real shock — Avouka went into receivership. Unsuspected by anybody, Mr Eidess was a heavy gambler, and had misappropriated large sums of money. A lot of work waiting to be finished and even some advance orders had already been paid for by customers, but the money had disappeared, together with Mr Eidess. The business folded, and I had no job. Luckily, one of the compositors at the parent business to Avouka, the Zionist daily *Undzer Vort*, was leaving for the USA at that time, and I was offered his position. That was a good break for me.

The second event was a very happy one. Since Fela had recovered from her illness, we had begun to look for an apartment in a more central position in Paris. Clichy, where we lived, was an outer suburb. We felt somehow cut off from Jewish social life, and from most of our friends, and it was also a little too far from my workplace. I sought the help of a Jewish middleman, who was active in the Belleville area of the 20th arrondissement. This time we had an asset, our apartment, which would help us to make up the necessary key-money.

Towards the end of December, we were offered an exceptional apartment on the third floor of a building that had been built just before the war, in 1938. It had facilities unheard of in Paris — central heating, a modern kitchen, a bathroom, and a separate toilet — but had been very run down by the previous, illegal tenant, and needed a good deal of redecorating. The building also had a lift. We could not believe that we were so lucky. There was a catch, of course. The current lessee, a survivor of Auschwitz, was not allowed to transfer the apartment to a new tenant. He had just gained possession of it again, after a long court battle with the previous tenant, who had lived there after the owner and his family were deported, in 1942. His wife and child had perished. By the time he got his apartment back, he had remarried, and lived with his new wife in her place.

In my presence, he told the landlord that we were just swapping apartments; it was too painful for him to live in his because it reminded him too much of his family. The landlord agreed immediately. I paid him a tiny transfer fee, and all the paperwork was done in a short time. We did not have to repeat the same phony story to my landlord, who was Jewish and understood our situation well. He knew that my apartment would be sold off to a new tenant immediately. After the official swap of apartments was accomplished, I was happy to pay the agreed extra sum of money, which was very reasonable. As a matter of fact, it was a bargain. It was our good fortune to have had an apartment that could be counted as part payment for the new one — otherwise we could never have afforded an apartment of such quality, in the heart of the Jewish area of Paris. We were the envy of all our friends.

In the middle of January 1950, we moved in to our new, completely redecorated apartment. The sanded and polished parquetry floors made us very proud. Although we were practically broke, we had to buy new furniture for the lounge-dining room. The store-owner accepted payment in twelve monthly instalments, without interest. We were extremely happy; I had a permanent, well-paid job, and could well afford it.

Living in the Belleville area made a great difference to us. We enjoyed being so close to everything. Travelling to work was a matter of a few minutes. Shopping became much easier for Fela. We went out to visit friends more often, and they reciprocated. The whole apartment block was full of Jewish tenants, so we had a lot of good neighbours. The centre strip of the wide Boulevard de Belleville was transformed every Saturday and Sunday into a street market. Stalls with every kind of food, clothing, and other merchandise lined both sides of the strip, and did excellent business. On Sunday mornings, it was usual for hundreds of the Jewish post-war arrivals, many of them accompanied by young children, to stroll on the footpath, up and down the boulevard. People who worked hard during the week met their friends there; some became embroiled in heated political discussions, while others concluded business deals. Life was never dull in the centre of the Jewish Belleville area. Henri, whom we enrolled in a nearby kindergarten, also liked our new surroundings.

My two sisters, Rose and Maria, whom I had not seen since 1939, wrote to us often from Sweden. They both still lived in the town of Norrköping. Rose was still single, but Maria had been married since 1946, and she had a daughter, Yvonne, a little older than Henri. They both longed to see us and our son, as much as we wanted to see them. Sometime in late spring 1950, Rose wrote to us that at last she was able to fulfil her wish to visit us — she would come to Paris in July, and could stay with us for two months. Of course, we were delighted. Rose was not only my sister, but she was also Fela's best friend. As for Henri, who had never known a relative before, he became very impatient, and kept on talking about how he would welcome his aunty.

As summer approached, Fela made arrangements with Regina Besserman to spend the holiday period together near Rambouillet, the town where the French president had his summer palace, about ninety kilometres from the famous chateau and forest of Fontainebleau. They rented rooms in a large farmhouse that accommodated city people during the summer school holidays. As was common among Jewish working people in Paris, the women and children usually stayed there from the end of June until the end of August. The husbands, who had to keep on working, would come for the weekends, and the lucky ones, who got their annual leave in that period, would spend it there with their families. My annual leave was not due until the end of the year, but I was happy that Fela and Henri would spend the summer away from the stifling heat of Paris, with Regina and her son, Roger, who was nearly the same age as our son.

We ordered a sofa bed for Rose, and put it in our lounge room. We also made sure that there was enough room to accommodate Rose in our holiday place. As planned, Fela and Henri went to Rambouillet, and remained there. It was a beautiful area, the weather was good, and they had a lovely time. The two boys, Henri and Roger, were good friends, and enjoyed each other's company as much as their mothers enjoyed each other's. I did not mind travelling to Rambouillet every Saturday morning and returning to Paris on Sunday afternoon. During the week, I worked in Paris, and eagerly looked forward to Saturday, when I would again join my family for the precious weekend.

Of the five men working on our daily, four had their wives staying in the country over the summer. Living on our own during the week, each of us improvised as best as he could. Some cooked for themselves at home; others, like me, became regulars at a nearby small restaurant, where the owners treated us as members of their own family.

One day, one of my co-workers proposed that all of us should go out the following evening, after work, to have dinner at a small nightclub in Pigalle, the red-light district of Paris. He said that he knew the proprietor well, and assured us that we would not only have a good meal, but we would also enjoy a good night out. We all agreed. As for myself, I was not particularly happy with the idea, but I had to go along with the others.

So, on a lovely summer evening, we followed our leader to the Pigalle nightclub. As we entered, a few couples were already dancing to the intimate beat of a tango. We were met by the owner, and as soon as we sat down, champagne bottles appeared on the table. We drank and ate and became merry. A young lady suddenly appeared beside each of us, to keep us company and to share our champagne. Later, my companion invited me to dance with her, and I accepted with great gusto. However, after only a few steps, I had a complete blackout and dropped to the floor.

I woke up in a dry bathtub, but not alone. Alongside my head was a pair of feet belonging to one of my workmates. We both were adventurers of a small calibre, and had spent the night in the tub. When I came to Rambouillet on the following Saturday, I told Fela the whole story — the truth and nothing but the truth. She just smiled, and said that I deserved a much harsher punishment, because I had intended to sin.

Regina's husband, Yanek, was a fanatical communist, as were all their relatives. At the holiday place where we stayed with them, there was a group of their friends who were also communists. Yanek himself had left Poland and gone to Spain during the Civil War in 1936. He had joined the Polish unit, the Dąbrowski Brigade, and fought against Franco's army and their allies until the Republic's defeat in 1939. He had then fled to France and had stayed there until 1941, when he was interned by the Germans as a Polish communist.

Yanek was deported and survived Auschwitz. He returned to Paris after the liberation, and later married Regina, whose brother was a good comrade of his. Yanek remained a steadfast party man who saw the Soviet Union as a model of the bright future awaiting mankind under communism.

The weekends in Rambouillet were not just about relaxation and family reunions. When the men got together, the political events of the past week were reviewed. Any wrongs, wherever they happened in the world, were invariably attributed to the war-mongering Americans. Anything positive, on the other hand, was credited to the great Soviet Union.

At the time, serious questions were being asked about the fate of Yiddish writers and Jewish culture in general in the Soviet Union. The minute I opened my mouth about that subject, I was accused of being an anti-Soviet, fascist lackey — a scaremonger. It was not possible to argue with them. They claimed that nowhere else in the world had Jews had as much freedom as in the Soviet Union.

Years later, when we visited Regina and Yanek in Paris in 1985, Yanek was a different person. Gone was his harshness, abrasiveness, and aggressive manner. The passing years and political upheavals had mellowed him considerably. He had become very conservative in his views, and even accused his son, Roger, of being too radical, of not understanding the situation of Israel, and of ignoring the specific needs of the Jewish people. It was quite amusing to listen to the new Yanek. He died in Paris, in 1987.

At last, at the end of July, Rose arrived from Sweden. In fact, there was a mix-up about her exact arrival time. I had just come from the country on that Sunday afternoon, and had planned to meet her at the railway station at the time the train was due to arrive. To my great surprise, Rose was waiting for me in the concierge's apartment, having arrived a couple of hours earlier than planned. The good lady concierge knew that I was awaiting a visitor from Sweden, and had been very helpful to Rose, with whom she had to communicate in sign language.

Our joy was great. After nearly eleven years, we had finally met again. A lot had happened in the meantime. We had parted as adolescents, and now we were adults. I left Rose in the apartment and went to work; it was a Sunday, but a normal working day for me.

That night, we talked and talked until morning. What I remember mostly is one particular detail about our parents. Rose told me how, during the terrible years in the ghetto, they had repeated on many occasions that they were happy that I had escaped from the Germans. Despite the pain of being separated from their only son, they were convinced that I had done the right thing and that I would survive.

Rose was very anxious to meet Fela and Henri as soon as possible. In the morning, I took her to Rambouillet. There was great joy in the family. Rose and Fela had a lot to talk about. They were not just sisters-in-law; they had been the closest of friends before the war. The last time they had met was in August 1944 in Auschwitz, in horrible circumstances. As for Henri, he was absolutely delighted, and kept on talking to his aunty in fluent Yiddish. At the end of August, Fela, Henri, and Rose came back to Paris. They had all had a lovely time in Rambouillet, and looked healthy and suntanned.

Every day, friends dropped in to our apartment to meet my sister. On other occasions, Rose went to visit her pre-war acquaintances who were living in Paris at the time. During the week, and on the weekends, we went out with Rose as often as we could. On many occasions, Rose and young Henri — who adored her — went out by themselves with Henri acting as an interpreter. We hoped that Rose would meet a suitable man in Paris, that she would get married and remain near us. She wanted that, too, but somehow it did not work out that way. Rose prolonged her visa and stayed with us for three months. In the end, she had to go back to Sweden, alone.

For some time, I had been wanting to test my entrepreneurial abilities, as well as earn some additional income. I worked in the afternoons, and could devote my entire mornings to that purpose. I began to look for orders for printing jobs. I planned to prepare the work and then have it printed at a firm whose proprietor was very friendly and encouraging towards me in regards to my new venture. I picked up a few orders from business firms and organisations, and I had no trouble delivering them on time. At that point, I was given the chance to finish a very large job, a Yiddish translation of a tractate from the Babylonian Talmud.*

---

* The Talmud is a compilation of the teachings and opinions of a wide range of scholars around texts in the Jewish Bible. It was put together during the period 200–500CE, and serves as the basis of Jewish law. Talmudic writings were collected from both Palestinian and Babylonian sources, with the Babylonian Talmud normally carrying greater weight. The Talmud is divided into 63 tractates, each on a particular subject area.

A Belgian Jew, a jeweller, had made a vow during the war, while hiding from the Germans in France. He had vowed that if he survived the war, he would finance the publication of a Yiddish translation of five Talmudic tractates, including the original Aramaic and Hebrew text, and the Rashi commentaries.** He survived, and began to prosper financially. He found a suitably educated person, a rabbi, to work on the project for a few years. Finally, when the translation was ready, the jeweller, called Levkovitz, could not find a Jewish printery in Brussels capable of producing that kind of work. So Levkovitz went to Paris, to see the typesetters of *Undzer Vort*, and the linotype operators there accepted his order to prepare the Yiddish setting for the first of the tractates, the *Bava Kamma*. One of the compositors — the one whom I eventually replaced when he left Paris — was going to combine, on each large page of the tractate, the setting of the Yiddish text with photo blocks of the original text and Rashi commentaries.

By the time I was approached by Mr Levkovitz, the blocks and the metal of the partially set first tractate had been lying around, untouched, for a long time. Not one page had been made up or proofed. I was recommended to Mr Levkovitz as the only person who could make up the pages and supervise the printing, as well as the binding, of the first

---

** Rashi is the commonly used acronym for Rabbi Shlomo Yitzhaki (1040–1105), the pre-eminent commentator on the Jewish Bible and Talmud who was based in the French town of Troyes. All editions of the Babylonian Talmud for the last 500 years have included Rashi's commentaries in their margins.

tractate. Mr Levkovitz was an extremely likeable and honest person. He understood how difficult and time-consuming the task of producing the tractate would be, and put me in touch with a person who would proof-read the pages. He promised to pay me well for my efforts, and offered me a completely free hand to proceed with the project.

I accepted the challenge, and set to work immediately. The job was even more difficult and slower going than I had thought. No one had planned or looked after the setting before. Consequently, a lot of the already-set manuscript had been done to wrong measures and had to be reset. There were numerous obstacles to overcome as I made up page after page. As soon as I got a section of the tractate completed, proofread, and approved, I proceeded to print it, on a special paper stock, which I had ordered as soon as I accepted the job. That way, Mr Levkovitz could follow our progress, however slow it was. He was a real gentleman, and truly appreciated my effort. He honoured our agreement and paid me promptly, as soon as I presented him with an account. As the year 1950 came to a close, nearly half of the tractate was finished.

Chapter Fifteen

DURING THE YEARS 1948 and 1949, the cold war, which had split the victorious anti-German allies of World War II into two blocs, progressively intensified. Nowhere else was the huge ideological gulf between the two camps felt as intensely as in Paris, the nerve centre of Europe, where the Communist Party had a huge following. The large headlines of the daily newspapers made one feel that a war between the two adversaries, the Soviet Union and its satellites on one side, and the USA with the Western democracies on the other, was unavoidable. In the highly charged political atmosphere of that time, tensions rose even higher when the communist daily, *L'Humanité*, openly proclaimed that, should there be a war, they, the French communists, would call on the people not to fight against the Soviet Union.

Jews who had arrived after the war, the majority of them survivors of Nazi camps or exile in the Soviet Union, again felt insecure. They did not want to live through another war — the last one had been more than enough for one lifetime. The poor accommodation in which most of them lived in Paris also played an important part in their decisions to leave.

Many of our friends decided to emigrate, mostly to Canada and Australia — the two countries actively inviting large-scale immigration of refugees.

The Jewish welfare organisations in both of those countries helped greatly by sponsoring potential Jewish migrants. The paperwork involved was minimal. One only had to apply for a landing permit, and wait a few months for a reply. A notification from the respective embassy, inviting the prospective immigrant to attend for a medical examination, usually arrived afterwards. As long as the applicant and his family were healthy, the permit was granted promptly. Then it was just a matter of waiting for an assigned berth on a ship. The fares were paid for by the United Nations' International Refugee Organisation or by the Joint.

The trickle of departures gained momentum after June 1950, when the cold war was suddenly transformed into a real war, in Korea. In a surprise move, the North Korean army crossed the 38th parallel and invaded South Korea. Within a short time, two huge armies were fighting each other, resulting in horrendous human losses on both sides. Millions of ordinary people — men, women, and children who were fleeing the battle zones and choking the roads of the devastated country — were also suffering terrible casualties. The survivors were becoming homeless refugees. It looked to us like an exact repetition of 1936, when the civil war in Spain, which went on for three years, proved itself to be a prologue of World War II.

More and more people opted to leave France. Encouraging letters from relatives and friends, who had left earlier, influenced their decision to emigrate. One after another, many of our friends and acquaintances left Paris; the majority of them went to Australia. Among them were a couple of my fellow printing tradesmen. They wrote to us in glowing terms about their new country. Of course, life was not easy for a newcomer, but it was a land of plenty. It had a warm climate, jobs were available for anyone willing to work, and it was peaceful — it had never in its history experienced war on its soil — and the opportunities for the future were unlimited.

Early in 1951, after General MacArthur, the commander of the US forces in Korea, asked President Truman for permission to blockade China's coastline and to bomb the Chinese bases in Manchuria, with atomic weapons if necessary, the world looked to be on the brink of a disastrous confrontation. The trickle of departures from Paris, which had already intensified in the previous year, became a veritable flood.

We were in a dilemma: we loved Paris and we were happy there; we had a beautiful apartment; I had a good job; and I was earning plenty of extra money, too. However, the political situation made us jittery. Fela, especially, was frightened of another war. We also had to take into consideration our son's future. Even the thought that we might be caught up in a war again made us look seriously at the idea of emigration. However, it was too difficult to decide — until then, we had never even contemplated leaving France. We talked about it a lot, assessed the pros and cons, but could not make up our minds.

I continued my daily routine. In the mornings, I was busy with the *Bava Kamma* tractate. I tried to speed up its completion, but the job was of a particularly difficult nature; it demanded a great deal of attention to detail. In the afternoons, I worked my normal shift on the Yiddish daily. Towards the end of April, my sister Maria wrote to me that she, her husband, Åke, and their four-year-old daughter, Yvonne, would like to visit us in June. She knew that we might not remain in France, and she did not want to delay our get-together any longer. We were delighted with the news.

The war in Korea continued, minus General MacArthur, who was relieved of his command by President Truman in April. Fela and I were still undecided about migrating from France. Just before my sister's arrival, we came upon a clever idea: we would apply for landing permits for both Australia and Canada, as a kind of insurance against whatever might happen. This allowed us to postpone our final decision.

Maria, Åke, and Yvonne arrived by train in the middle of June 1951. Our joy was great when we met each other at the railway station. Instead of the thirteen-year-old girl whom I had known when I left home in 1939, Maria was now a young woman of twenty-five, with a husband and young daughter. Åke was obviously a little shy at first, but he spoke some German and soon joined us in the chaotic shouting, laughing, and shedding of a few tears of happiness. The children were bewildered — they could not understand each other. Yvonne did not speak Yiddish, only Swedish, which Henri did not understand. He was disappointed, but they somehow got their conversation going in sign language.

Later, we sat down to a welcome dinner in our apartment, around a beautifully prepared table. Fela had excelled herself to make the occasion a memorable one. The party atmosphere continued for the whole length of their visit. Coming from an, in some ways, austere Sweden, our guests were especially overwhelmed by the quality and quantity of the alcoholic beverages we offered them. (Once, my brother-in-law quietly asked me how I could afford all those drinks. I assured him that he did not have to worry about it.)

Our guests remained with us for twelve days. They met a lot of our friends, whom we invited to our place daily to share our joy. They simply loved Paris, and wanted to see as much of it as was possible. Because I worked at a daily newspaper and there was no one to replace me, I had to be away in the afternoons and evenings. Whenever I could not accompany them, our guests went out with Fela and Henri. The two young cousins became very friendly during that time. On some occasions, Åke and Maria went out by themselves. Åke was very smart, and he easily found his own way around Paris. We got on very well with our guests. They were not just our relatives; we became good friends, too. When they left us, we all knew that our warm family relationship and friendship would last forever.

In September, we were called for medical examinations, first to the Canadian and then to the Australian embassy. Fela, myself, and Henri easily passed both medicals, and landing permits were offered to us by each of those countries. By that time, our mind was made up. Although the war in Korea was momentarily at a standstill, the threat of a global conflict was still very real. Many more post-war arrivals had left France by then.

After consulting my sister Rose, who advised us of her preference for Australia, and said that she would join us there later, we decided to emigrate to Australia — the country furthest away from previous wars, the country where many of our friends had settled and where we, too, would build a future for ourselves.

We began to prepare for departure. First of all, I had to finish the *Baba Kama*, which I did in good time. At the end of November, the last sheet rolled off the press and I sent it to the bookbinders with appropriate binding instructions. A very happy Mr Levkovitz came over from Brussels. He thanked me for what I had accomplished, generously settled the account, and wished me and my family good luck for the future. He also promised to send me a bound volume in which my effort was acknowledged, to our new address in Australia. He was a man of honour and kept his promise, as always.

The second, even more important, task before us was to find a new tenant for our apartment quietly, without attracting unwanted attention. Luck was on our side. A young French-Jewish family who had returned from the United States, which they had not found to their liking, offered to take over our apartment with all its contents —

privately, without a middleman. Their offer of 1,500 American dollars was more than we had hoped for. Even more importantly, they agreed to move in after we had departed, and only then attend to the paperwork with the landlord. The young man was a French citizen, a war-orphan and, as a son of war-deportees, was entitled to special privileges.

We had successfully accomplished the two important tasks. While waiting for a notification of transport, we began to prepare for our departure in earnest. I gave notice of my impending departure to my employers, with whom I had a very friendly relationship. Then, acting on advice from my colleagues in Australia, I requested and obtained a membership card from the French printing union. I was advised that possessing such a card would save me a lot of trouble getting a job in the highly unionised printing industry in Australia.

One practical problem we wrestled with was how much clothing and which household items we should include in our luggage. As it happened, the advice we received was incorrect, and we ordered too much hand-tailored clothing for each of us. The money spent on it would have been of much more use to us in Australia. In the middle of December, we received all the necessary documents. Our assigned ship, *Cyrenia*, would sail from Genoa on 22 December. We had to leave Paris, by overnight express train, on 20 December 1951.

We bade goodbye to Paris with mixed feelings. We were deserting a city that we really loved. However, it was too late for regrets. One thing was sure, though: we were leaving Paris richer than we had been when we entered it in March 1947. We now had a son of four, and over 1,200 American dollars in our pockets. We arrived in Genoa on the 21st, at midday, and were led to a hotel for an overnight stay. On the afternoon of the 22nd, we embarked on the *Cyrenia*, a Greek-owned vessel that had served as a hospital ship during World War II, nearing the end of her usefulness, but good enough to shuttle migrants from Europe to Australia.

It was one-class accommodation only — the lowest. Men and women, even families, were separated. Except for young babies, which were allowed to remain with their mothers, boys had to be with their fathers and girls with their mothers, in cabins holding four persons each. Families met on deck, when possible, and in the dining room, which had two sittings for every meal. The food during the voyage was barely edible and too oily, but there was plenty of it for people who could digest it. Henri was one of them — he just loved the pasta.

The sea voyage was quite pleasant. Half of the passengers were Jews, from different places in Europe: Poland, German DP camps, Belgium, France, and Italy. We got to know a great number of people, and became friendly with many of them. There were lots of children, too, and Henri had plenty of playmates. A Lebanese man on board, a Christian, offered to teach English in small classes to anybody willing to learn, at no cost. I enrolled immediately, and learned many basic English expressions, which was to help me a great deal during our first weeks in Australia.

We passed through the Suez Canal and proceeded to Aden, then Colombo. The next stop was Fremantle, Western Australia, where we were allowed to leave the ship and wander through the port city. It was a hot January day, and I was very thirsty. In a corner pub, I had my first taste of Australian beer — it was delicious. After a while, the ship left Fremantle for our destination, Melbourne. The passage through the notoriously stormy seas of the Great Australian Bight was the worst of the whole voyage. We were all seasick. Our ship was thrown around by huge waves, like a matchbox. The dining room was empty — for two days, very few people needed feeding. At last, the storm abated, the sea became calm, and everyone was in a good mood when we docked at Station Pier, in Port Melbourne, on 17 January 1952.

Chapter Sixteen

AFTER GOING THROUGH the usual customs and immigration formalities, we stepped ashore with our luggage on a hot January afternoon. Many of the new arrivals were met by relatives who had already prepared accommodation for them. We were not that lucky. However, three of our friends were waiting to welcome us, and that lifted our spirits. They gave us some practical tips and promised to come to see us very soon at the migrant reception centre of the Jewish Welfare and Relief Society, where we would be staying temporarily. The welfare society, whose officers were mostly volunteers, did a terrific job for the masses of Jewish migrants who were constantly arriving in Melbourne. Their reception centre was of particular benefit to people like us.

One of our friends advised me that I could get a job immediately. However, we had to find private accommodation first. The reception centre was crowded, and there was obviously no privacy in such a place. We were luckier than many other people who had arrived without any money — they had no other option, and depended solely on accommodation provided by the welfare society. After a few days at the centre, we accepted an offer from a migrant family who had just bought a house: for a weekly rent of £5 we could have the front bedroom, and could share all the facilities of the house.

Our first address in Melbourne was Rennie Street, Thornbury. On the morning after we moved in, I went to look for a job. I bought an *Age* newspaper and marked a few advertisements from the 'Situations Vacant' columns. The first place I walked in to was Perfection Press, in Gertrude Street, Fitzroy. It was only about six kilometres from where we lived, on the same tram route.

My English was not very good, but Mr Gilmour, the owner, knew a few French words, and guessed that I was after the advertised compositor's job. He invited me into the composing room, and once there I easily convinced him that I could do any job, even in English. I stayed on working until mid-afternoon, when Mr Gilmour told me that I could have the job and that I would earn £15 per week. Then he said he wanted to meet my family, and gave me a ride home in his car. The day's try-out was considered a full day's work at my first job in Australia.

When we decided to leave Paris and emigrate to Australia, we knew that we would have to start from scratch again. We expected it to be tough. However, the reality was even tougher. Instead of the beautiful, fully furnished apartment we had had in Paris, we became lodgers. Despite paying high rent, we were dependent on the owner-occupiers for when we could use the bathroom, the kitchen, or the laundry. The situation was especially depressing for Fela, who had to put up with all the niggling day-to-day irritations. During the first few weeks, I found her crying silently on many occasions. I understood her well. I was not happy either, yet there was no turning back. We had to establish ourselves here; we simply had to succeed.

Our first goal was to be living on our own. There were two available options: buying a house or renting an apartment, which also meant paying substantial key-money. We preferred buying, building up an asset. Our whole capital of US$1,200 (changed to around £600) was not quite enough for a deposit on a decent house. We somehow had to save some more money in a hurry. My wage was enough to live on, but did not leave too much for savings. The only way out was for Fela to find a paying job — something she had never had to do in France.

Firstly, we had to work out who would look after Henri, now called Henry, while she was at work. Our landlady solved the problem for us. She advised Fela to enrol four-year-old Henry immediately, as a five-year old, at the primary school, which her son, who was a little older than Henry, had been attending for some time. She assured Fela that, because Henry was a tall boy, no one would suspect that Fela had lied about his age. The lady offered to take both boys to and from school in the mornings and afternoons, and to look after Henry until Fela came home from work. Fela followed the advice of our hostess, and Henry was accepted at the school without any difficulty. Then she went to a clothing factory to learn hand-finishing.

After four weeks at Perfection Press, I had to leave. Although the owner was happy with my work, the foreman, who was not a very friendly person, kept on niggling me. According to him, I was working too fast or did things differently from how he had told me. He knew that I was a much better tradesman than him, and probably feared that I would be a threat to his position. Anyway, I was not prepared to put up with the man. I gave notice to a very unhappy Mr Gilmour and found myself another, better-paying, job in the city. It was at a typesetting and stereotyping firm, which worked only for advertising agencies. They had a composing room, staffed by five people, to make-up press advertisements. Then they produced duplicates in their stereotyping department and distributed them to newspapers all over the continent.

Poor Henry came home in tears after his first day at school. The children had teased him, calling him 'Frenchy', and he could not answer — he did not understand them because they were talking to him in English. However, Henry was so smart that after two months he could speak English as well as, if not better than, the other children in his class. He even became the teacher's assistant. If the teacher had to leave the class for a short time, he would ask Henry to deputise for him.

Whenever I was offered overtime work, I accepted it gladly. Fela did her best, too, and she was earning some money at the clothing factory. We wanted to buy a house as soon as we could afford it. One day, we had a visitor. Laybl Herszberg came to see us. The Herszbergs had arrived in Sydney late in 1947, and had settled in well. We had not seen them since the end of July 1946, before our departure from Lodz, when Fela Herszberg had been expecting the birth of her first child within weeks. Now she was the mother of three sons.

We were genuinely pleased that Laybl had come to see us. His wife had prompted him to visit us at the first opportunity. The Herszbergs proved themselves to be real friends. They were genuinely happy that we had come to Australia, and gave us a lot of encouragement. Laybl assured us that we would do well. As he put it, it was just a matter of overcoming teething troubles. He agreed with us that we should buy a house without delay and, what was more important, he offered us a modest loan if we needed it.

In April, we did just that. We bought a new, two-bedroom, weatherboard house in a newly developing neighbourhood in Pascoe Vale South — at 31 Rainer Street, off Moreland Road. It was on the crest of a hill, overlooking the Essendon valley, in the municipality of Coburg. The area was served by a direct tram route to the city and two private bus lines. The price was £3,100, on a deposit of £800. We bought it directly from the builder, who agreed to finance it himself, on a five-year term, at 4.5 per cent interest, with repayments of £65 per quarter (£5 per week). Four months after our arrival in Australia, we had joined the landowner class of the country!

After paying the agreed deposit and the lawyer's fees, including adjustments to the rates, we had very little money left for furniture and all the other necessary household goods. Previously, we had bought a bed and mattress for Henry and a mattress for ourselves. When we moved into our new house early in June, we decided that there were two items of furniture we had to buy immediately — a bedroom suite for ourselves and a kitchen table with four chairs. Everything else, including floor coverings, would have to wait. We would even have to do without a refrigerator — an ice-box was all we could afford.

I looked into the Saturday *Age* advertisements and found a three-piece bedroom suite, offered for £35. It was just right for us — our finances would not allow for anything dearer. I bought it, and got it delivered for 30 shillings. Then we bought the cheapest possible kitchen table with four matching chairs. The price of the bedroom suite was very low, but the quality of it was even lower. It took us some time to get used to the bed. It was so fragile that we were afraid it would buckle under our weight — it creaked and squeaked at the slightest movement of our bodies. The small wardrobe had doors that would not stay closed, and the dressing-table mirror was always leaning to one side. The kitchen table and the chairs, however, were not bad at all. As for our lounge room, where we would have to entertain all our expected visitors, we put our large shipping trunk in the centre of the room and six empty fruit boxes around it, to sit on.

Despite all these shortcomings, we were happy — we had begun to strike roots in Australia. We enrolled Henry at the Coburg West Primary School, which was on a direct bus route from the bus-stop near our house. Although he had not yet reached his fifth birthday, Henry was a sensible and clever boy, quite capable of travelling to and from his school by himself. The change of school had no negative effect on his education at all. There were also a few other Jewish children at the school; one of them, Gerry Grokop, was the son of a camp-mate of mine who lived in West Coburg.

Our whole neighbourhood was settled by young couples with children, many of them Henry's age. There were still a lot of vacant blocks around, so the youngsters had a wonderful time. If he came home from school before his mother had arrived from work, Henry had friends and playmates to pass the time with. As well, when the weather was bad, he could always go to a neighbour's house — he was liked by all of them, and they showed great friendliness to us.

Each of the neighbours took it on himself to advise me how to establish our garden: how to prepare the soil for a lawn, which shrubs to plant, and how to use the backyard for vegetables. I was a good listener. So well did I learn that in the first summer of 1952–1953 we had a crop of all sorts of vegetables. As for tomatoes, we had so many that we could offer them to all our friends.

I was happy at work. The owner, Mr Odgers, was a decent and a fair-minded man. The manager, a Scot, who had served with Mr Odgers in the air force during the war, was also a pleasant man. It was a small composing room, and the five of us got on well. After work, they all usually went to the nearby pub for a few drinks. For the first two days I went with them, but I soon realised that I could not keep up with their drinking habits. After two beers, I had had enough —

and they had just begun. So I told them truthfully that in the future I could not join them for drinks. They understood me well, and never criticised me for not coming with them.

One day, Mr Odgers asked me if I would like to accompany him to a wine tasting, at a city merchant's cellar. He assumed that, having lived in France for so many years, I was an expert in the field. He explained that his wife wanted to show her guests how sophisticated her taste in wine was. He then told me honestly that he himself did not understand a thing about wine, and therefore he would rely on me to pick some good ones. We moved along the well-stocked tables, tasting as many as we could. I did my best to choose a number of good wines. Whatever I chose, Mr Odgers bought — two dozen of each, one for himself and one for me. He put the lot in his large Buick trunk, and after work he drove me home. As the greatly surprised Fela and Henry looked on, we unloaded the boxes of wine — my share of the proceedings.

I was being paid good wages, but, even with some overtime and with Fela's extra earnings, we could only just cover our expenses. We simply needed too many things at once. Towards the end of the year, Mr Odgers called me to his office and told me that the position of foreman had become vacant. He explained that the man who held that job for some time was an alcoholic and that he, Mr Odgers, could not put up with his absences from work anymore. I was offered the job at once. Mr Odgers assured me that he and the manager had full confidence in my ability to do the job well. He added that he was not concerned about my temporary linguistic shortcomings, as far as the English language was concerned. Understandably, my wages would also improve. After consulting Fela, I accepted the challenge. In fact, I had run the composing room on many occasions previously, whenever the foreman had had a bad hangover from one of his regular drinking binges.

The year 1953 began well enough for us. We settled into a routine and worked very hard, but we did not mind that. Fela attended to her housework after she came home from work, and I used every spare minute at home to get our garden into better shape. Henry was happy, and continued to do very well at school. He was very understanding for his age and never too demanding. We decided to break our principle of not buying anything on hire-purchase, and ordered a refrigerator. We just could not wait until we had saved the necessary cash for it.

No matter how busy we were, we did not neglect our social contacts. We often welcomed friends in our house, and we reciprocated, too, mostly on weekends. The few Jewish families living in our neighbourhood quickly established good relationships among themselves and dropped in to each other's places whenever possible. As well, I attended all the Bund party meetings, and our family never failed to be present at functions held in the Kadimah cultural centre — the best occasions to meet many of the post-war Jewish immigrants.

During that summer, Henry got very excited when I told him that we were going by car to the seaside village of San

Remo on the following Sunday. My employer, Mr Odgers, who wanted the families of his managerial staff to get together, organised the outing. The participants were to be Mr Odgers and his wife; the manager, Jock Hall, and his wife and young son; and the stereotyping department foreman, Freddie, and his wife. Fela, Henry, and I were invited to join them, and the three of us were to travel in Mr Odger's Buick.

On a warm late-February morning, we travelled by tram to the assembly point in East Malvern, the residence of Mr and Mrs Odgers. Very soon, the other cars arrived and we set out on the trip, following each other. I was surprised when we all stopped at a country pub, not far past Dandenong.[*] Everyone went inside, and it was soon evident that the publican was a good mate of Mr Odgers, who had just dropped in to say hello to his friend. Of course, the men in our party had a few beers, and the ladies and children ordered soft drinks.

After a while we hit the road again, but we had not travelled very far before we stopped in front of another pub. It was a repetition of the first stop — the publican was another mate of Mr Odgers. We made a third stop on the way before we finally arrived at San Remo in the afternoon. By that time, the kids were very hungry, so the ladies, the children, and I quickly sat down to a picnic lunch at the nearby beach. The other men went to the pub to say hello to their mate, the publican, and naturally to have a few beers.

---

* This was barely one-quarter of the way to their destination.

After lunch, the children went for a dip in the sea, the ladies got to know each other, and I wandered around the fishing village for a while. A little later, I entered the pub, to see how my friends were doing. They were just fine. As a matter of fact, they were finishing their last drink, they told me, but it was getting late and it was time to go home. Before we did that, Mr Odgers bought a couple of large crayfish and invited us to stay for dinner at his place. By the time we arrived there, it was getting dark. We had a lovely dinner, and afterwards Mr Odgers offered to drive us home. It was late in the evening, and Henry was fast asleep in the car when we reached our home. We had experienced our first typical Australian summer outing.

In the autumn, Fela suddenly became ill. Our local doctor, Mr Percy Zerman, diagnosed the illness as glandular fever, a serious and debilitating disease. He told me that Fela would have to stay in bed for a few weeks, and she would need constant care. I found myself in a very difficult situation. I could take only a few days off work. Henry, although very understanding and helpful, still had to be looked after. We had no relatives to turn to, and our friends lived too far away to be of any real help. It was then that we were shown real human kindness.

Our next-door neighbours, the Roach family, were an example of true, old-fashioned Australian mateship. As soon as she heard about our situation, Mrs Roach volunteered to care for Fela and to look after Henry after he returned from school. Then there was Mrs Zerman, the wife of our doctor, who dropped in a few times during the following days, while I was away at work, to make sure that Fela was comfortable. As well, there was the Muscatel family, with whom we had travelled from Paris to Australia. They lived not far from us, and we were quite friendly with them. Mrs Muscatel came to see Fela every day, brought her some delicacies, and insisted that Henry and I have dinner with them on numerous occasions. We were lucky. Fela got better sooner than expected, and happiness reigned again in our family.

The year 1953 was moving to its end. As we had suspected would happen, my sister Rose did not join us in Australia. Instead, she was going to Canada, where she was to marry Sam Neiman, a man she had known for many years in Sweden. Sam had a brother in Toronto, and had gone there ahead of Rose. We were very delighted by the news, and wished them both a happy and joyful married life. Although Canada was so far from us, it would not stop us meeting each other in the future. We were sure of that.

For some time, Fela had hinted to me that she wanted another child. Henry often asked us why he could not have a little brother, like most of his friends. He even proposed to forego his pocket money, so we could buy him a baby brother. I wanted another child, too, but perhaps a little later, after our financial situation had improved. Anyway, early in 1954, Fela told me happily that she was pregnant. My uncertainty evaporated instantly, and I was happy, too.

Fela felt terrific, and did not take any special care. She continued to rush off to work in the morning and to rush back home in the afternoon, to begin her usual house work. As a consequence, she miscarried, in the third month of the pregnancy. We were both devastated. Fela promised me that when she became pregnant next time, hopefully soon, she would look after herself a lot more, from the beginning until the birth of the baby.

Fela had first become aware of the possibility of restitution payments from the West German government while we were still living in France. By 1952, the West Germans had agreed to make payments to all eligible former inmates of ghettos and camps. The formalities dragged on for years. During 1954, an Australian-Jewish lawyer began pushing Fela's case. More documents and certificates were requested by the German authorities. In the end, Fela's camp-sister, Regina Besserman, came to our rescue. From Paris, she was able to obtain all the necessary medical certificates from the Clichy hospital and from her private doctor. Fela's lawyer thought that this time the Germans would not be able to delay settling her case for much longer. We would just have to be patient a little longer.

As the year 1955 began, we hoped for better times. We would somehow have to buy a car, too, although we did not have the money to pay for it. The public and private transport that served our area was not bad, but it was slow, especially on the weekends, when we wanted to visit people. As well, we enrolled Henry in the I.L. Peretz Yiddish Sunday school in Carlton. Getting there on a Sunday morning and coming back home by public transport was both tedious and time-consuming.

Suddenly, everything changed for the better. Firstly, Fela was pregnant again. Conscious of what had happened last time, she immediately reduced her workload, and in general became a lot more careful, at all times. When she went for a medical examination, the doctor was very happy with her. He praised her and told her that she could expect the happy event of our baby's birth around 20 November. When he learned about it, Henry was the happiest boy in the neighbourhood; but he insisted, he wanted a little brother, not a sister.

Then the prediction of Fela's lawyer materialised. We were notified by him that the compensation payment to Fela, the so-called *Wiedergutmachung*, had at last been approved by the German authorities. The actual money, about £1,250, arrived not long afterwards. It was a huge sum of money for us; the equivalent of more than a year of my earnings, and it could not have come at a more opportune time. It did not take Fela very long to decide how to spend the money. We would buy a new washing machine and a new car — she did not trust any used machinery.

The washing machine was delivered to us and installed within a few days. As for the car, we decided on an English Hillman sedan and ordered one — but delivery was not expected for at least a month. That suited me well, since I had to get a driving licence first, and that was quite a task for me — I had never driven any vehicle in my life. The driving school I chose was recommended to me by friends. Its owner, a Jewish fellow, assured me that he would get me a licence before our car was ready to be picked up. He was true to his word. After about six lessons, I passed the driving test and received my licence. The problem was that although I was entitled to drive a car, that did not mean that I was actually able to drive it — at least not yet.

After work, on a Friday afternoon in the middle of September, I went to the city to pick up my new car from a showroom in Exhibition Street. I was not confident enough to drive through the city, so the salesman agreed to do it for me. He left me in Royal Parade, in the nearby suburb of Parkville, and I got behind the wheel. By the time I arrived home it was late, and Fela was very worried. I explained that I had had to drive slowly and carefully — that was the reason why it had taken me so long to come home. I promised Fela that I would bring her and our new baby home from hospital in our own car — I had two months left to gain experience in the art of driving.

Fela's pregnancy was progressing well. Although the doctor kept warning her that she was gaining too much weight and said that she should eat less, she had such an appetite that she just could not help herself. When she entered hospital on 21 November, the baby was a little overdue. She went into labour the next day, and she had a very tough time. The doctors wanted her to have a natural delivery, but the baby was too big. The following day, 23 November, I became very worried and did not leave the hospital. Fela was in great pain. She told me that she could not take any more and implored the chief obstetrician to take immediate action — she was afraid the baby would not survive any further delay. A little later, I was called into the office and asked to give my consent to a caesarean operation.

I was pacing the corridor outside the operating room, shocked and worried, when the smiling doctor came out and told me that everything was well. Fela had just given birth to a big and healthy boy. Before I left the hospital, I saw Fela and had a glimpse of the baby. They were both fine. I rushed to the Muscatels, where Henry was being looked after, to tell him the good news. His wish was fulfilled: he had a baby brother. We named the newborn after my father, Avrum Yoyne, but registered him under the equivalent English names of John Albert, following the advice of our good neighbour Mr Roach.**

Our old friend, Mr Herszberg, was ordered by his wife Fela to come over from Sydney to be with us at the circumcision ceremony, the *Bris-mile*. It took place at the hospital, and only a small group of friends and neighbours were invited. We really appreciated Laybl Herszberg's presence and his sharing of our joy on that memorable occasion. It was a sincere expression of his family's lasting friendship. Fela recuperated speedily, and after ten days she and the baby were ready to be taken home in our new car — driven by me, as promised.

Our family had grown. I was a father of two, and I had to earn enough by myself to provide for the family — Fela

---

** John's grandfather was usually called Yoyne.

would not be able to help out for at least two years. That was the immediate need, but I also had to plan for the future. Australia was a land of unlimited opportunity for anyone able and willing to put in the required effort. It was a country where all citizens were equal before the law and, what was even more important, where the immigrant was given a fair go. Encouraged by Fela, I hoped that in the future we would be able to establish our own business. Her enthusiasm and belief in my abilities was very contagious.

I had known for some time that I would have to change my job, which lately was not satisfying me anymore. This I did at the end of 1955. I went to work for the *Age* newspaper as a compositor, on the afternoon shift from 4.00 p.m. to 11.30 p.m. It suited me well to have the mornings free. I had found a rubber-stamp manufacturer in the city who offered me work every morning from 8.00 a.m. until noon, and all day on Saturdays. Of course, it meant long hours and it was tiring, but I did not mind that at all. I was young and healthy and, what was more important, I was earning enough to satisfy all the needs of our family. It also gave me a chance to save some money, which would certainly be needed if we were ever to start our own printing business.

In 1957, we sold our house in Pascoe Vale South, at a profit, and lived for a short time in rented premises in Carlton. At the time, we toyed with the idea of investing our money in a delicatessen. A number of Jewish newcomers owned such shops. They had to work very long hours, but they usually sold the business after keeping it for only a few years and ended up with a substantial profit. We thought we could do likewise. However, our good friend Laybl Herszberg was strongly against it, and talked us out of it. He reasoned that such a business was only good for people without a trade — I had a good trade, and should stick to it. He convinced us to drop the clever idea.

We bought a nice brick house in the suburb of Northcote, in Jenkins Street. It was a larger house than our previous one, on a very deep block with an established garden, and there was a bungalow in the backyard. We were close to public transport, and travelling to work by car, to the city, was also very convenient. We settled in well, and we were also lucky to have good neighbours there. The people next door, the Taylors, were very pleasant, and there were also a number of Jewish families living in our street and nearby. We became friendly with most of them.

Then I gave up my second job at the rubber-stamp manufacturer. Instead, I used the mornings to develop a gold-stamping service for shoe manufacturers — an idea that I had stumbled on by pure chance. Fela, with her usual common sense, was convinced that the new venture would hasten the realisation of our goal of establishing a printing business. She was very optimistic, and within a short time she had learned the whole operation of foil stamping on shoe uppers.

We rented small premises in the old industrial neighbourhood of Collingwood, the centre of the shoe trade. For the next two years, both of us worked long hours to fill the orders of our growing customer list. Fela did most of the actual work, while I made deliveries and pick-ups. Every day at 3.00 p.m. I would pick up young John from his kindergarten at the Peretz school in Carlton, bring him to Fela, then leave for the afternoon shift at the *Age*. Fela would close up after a while, then take a tram and bus to Northcote, to start her second shift — looking after the family and the home. As always, she remained the perfectionist and never complained.

By 1960, we had saved a sum of money and were ready to make the big move. I registered a printing business under the name of Globe Press, then I quit the *Age*. We rented larger premises, still in Collingwood, since we had to continue the gold-stamping service for some years to come. During that time, Fela had to be the bread-winner, while I put all my energy into establishing Globe Press Pty Ltd. It grew into a successful, medium-size printing company, with a very good reputation.

Our son Henry decided to join the company in 1976. A few years later, under his management, Globe Press Pty Ltd grew into a substantial book-printing company, owned by our family until it was sold in 1988.

Our faith in Australia was fully vindicated. The country was good to us. We fully appreciated the freedom, the rule of law, the egalitarian society, and the fairness with which we were treated. Our family found happiness here — as well, we raised two sons, of whom we are very proud. We also achieved independence and financial security. It certainly was not easy, but it has been well worth the effort.

Left: Fela, aged thirteen

Below: Fela (marked with x) with a group of girls, part of the 68 from the Lodz Ghetto *(Lohof, near Munich, 1942)*

Left: (clockwise) Mariem, Ruchl, Fishl, and Avrum Yoyne (*Lodz, 1925*)

Below: Fishl with some of his schoolmates (*Lodz, April 1936*)

Above: Ruchl (Rose), Malke (Maria), and Fishl (*Lodz, 1936*)

Rose (*Sweden, 1950*)

Maria (*Sweden, 1947*)

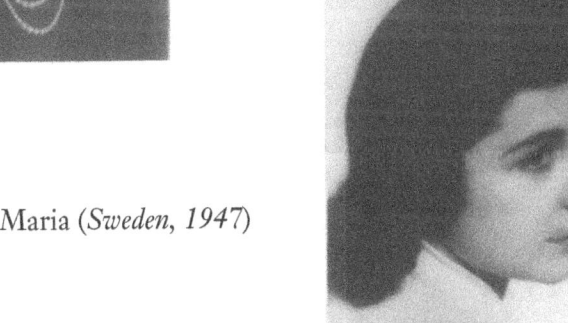

Above: Hanka and Szmulek Rozenblum, and Fela *(Lodz, 1946)*
Below: Henry and John *(Melbourne, 1957)*

Fela and Felix (*Alaska, 1982*)